Design for Water

Rainwater Harvesting, Stormwater Catchment, and Alternate Water Reuse

Design for Water

Rainwater Harvesting, Stormwater Catchment, and Alternate Water Reuse

Heather
Kinkade-Levario

NEW SOCIETY PUBLISHERS

Cataloging in Publication Data:
A catalog record for this publication is available from the National Library of Canada.

Cover design by Diane McIntosh. Leaf/waterdrop: iStock.
Inset photos: Heather Kinkade-Levario.

Printed in Canada.
Second printing November 2009.

Paperback ISBN: 978-0-86571-580-6

Inquiries regarding requests to reprint all or part of *Design for Water* should be addressed to New Society Publishers at the address below.

To order directly from the publishers, please call toll-free (North America) 1-800-567-6772, or order online at www.newsociety.com

Any other inquiries can be directed by mail to:

New Society Publishers
P.O. Box 189, Gabriola Island, BC V0R 1X0, Canada
1-800-567-6772

New Society Publishers' mission is to publish books that contribute in fundamental ways to building an ecologically sustainable and just society, and to do so with the least possible impact on the environment, in a manner that models this vision. We are committed to doing this not just through education, but through action. We are acting on our commitment to the world's remaining ancient forests by phasing out our paper supply from ancient forests worldwide. This book is one step toward ending global deforestation and climate change. It is printed on acid-free paper that is 100% old growth forest-free (100% post-consumer recycled), processed chlorine free, and printed with vegetable-based, low-VOC inks. For further information, or to browse our full list of books and purchase securely, visit our website at: www.newsociety.com

NEW SOCIETY PUBLISHERS   www.newsociety.com

Contents

Foreword

RAINWATER COLLECTION links human and environmental systems in mutually reinforcing health. On-site, it supports human life by, in effect, generating a new source of water. Upstream, it reduces the demand to develop off-site water supplies. Downstream, it protects water quantity and quality by reducing excess urban runoff and the associated pollution, erosion, and flooding. The technology and its applications are expanding and being refined. Its applicability to both arid and humid climates is becoming increasingly clear.

Heather Kinkade-Levario has made herself the leading expert in rainwater collection and its applications through a singular combination of systematic observation, focused academic study, and professional design experience. Her native area is the arid Southwest, where the need for water collection is most glaringly obvious and where the art of water catchment has devel-

oped most rapidly. She has been a leader in the American Rainwater Catchment Systems Association, the International Rainwater Catchment Systems Association, and the US Green Building Council.

Heather's first book on the subject—an award-winner in its own right—was published not long ago. But even since then, industry and design knowledge and applications have evolved and expanded. Advancements are being developed at home in North America, and introduced from Europe. Professional demands have risen for advanced technical information and new types of applications.

This new book raises available rainwater catchment, stormwater collection, and alternate water reuse information to the detailed technical level and broad scope of application required by professional architects, landscape architects, and engineers. It gives us clear writing, abundant case studies, great illustrations, and technical authority. It is organized, comprehensive, and accessible. Through it we see where and how rainwater catchment is being implemented and alternate water reused. We see at work both simple "passive" systems and the technically more demanding, but hydrologically much more complete and efficient, "active" systems. This new book elevates professionals' awareness and capability by providing the information they need. Immediately upon publication, it has the effect and stature of this growing technology's leading technical guideline and professional information resource.

— BRUCE K. FERGUSON, FASLA
Franklin Professor of Landscape Architecture and former
Director, University of Georgia School of Environmental Design
Author, *Stormwater Infiltration, Introduction to Stormwater, and Porous Pavements*

Preface

COLLECTING AND STORING rainwater is not a new idea. For almost 4000 years, cultures throughout the world have used captured rainwater. King Mesha of Moab won his war in his quest for land east of Jordan due to making reservoirs for catching water, the water that allowed him to survive through dry times. Wars have been fought and won over ownership of water or the ability to catch rainwater. It has even been said that water may be the oil of the 21st century. Continuing this thought today, collecting and using water more than one time can help reduce dependence on existing fresh water supplies. Much of the municipal water that has been purified to drinking water standards is used for tasks such as house cleaning, flushing toilets, gardening, and washing clothes or cars when drinking-water quality for these tasks is not required.

C. R. HATHCOCK

World Birding Center: One of 18 water tanks that store a total of 45,000 gallons

*World Birding Center:
Wildlife guzzler fed by an
adjacent rainwater tank*

Collecting rainwater, stormwater or an alternate water that has been used one time and can be used a second time with little or no treatment could provide a new water supply, saving the purified municipal water for high-quality water needs. Rainwater alone can help to improve poor-quality water, augment inefficient or undependable water supplies, cleanse soil by leaching built-up salt deposits, avoid the need for municipal chlorination and fluoridation treatments, and reduce or eliminate the cost of obtaining an alternate water supply. Drilling a well, laying a pipe for long distances, trenching in rocky conditions, or pumping water to higher elevations may prove to be too costly. In these and other instances, rainwater and stormwater collection as well as alternate water reuse can offer a more cost-effective water supply.

This potential supply of water is especially important in all arid and semi-arid regions where rainfall is neither frequent nor reliable. Collecting the water that falls onto a designated site then retaining that water and/or using water that is generated on site for on-site needs can be important for the sustainability of any design or development of a localized area. Applied consistently over the course of several projects, this water supply can have regional importance for the conservation of limited ground and surface water supplies.

Two water sources that potentially need very little filtration or purification are rainwater and fog condensate. However, both require specific techniques for collection. Fog collection, while it can only apply to specific elevations and geographic fog-producing features, requires large fog collection arrays, troughs, pipes,

*World Birding Center:
A 2,400-gallon tank*

*World Birding Center:
A tank next to the arched
roof catchment that feeds the
adjacent wildlife pond*

and water storage tanks. Similarly, the efficient collection of rainwater depends on several factors. First of all, the catchment area—the defined surface area upon which rainwater falls and is collected—should be carefully chosen. Pollutants introduced from a poorly chosen catchment area can affect the usability of the captured water. Second, the quantity of water to be collected, known as the rainwater harvesting potential, should be carefully evaluated. Third, the conveyance system that carries the water to storage must be designed, and an initial process of removing pollutants, known as a first-flush diversion or roof washing, must be considered. The water must also be stored and then distributed by gravity or by pumping.

Stormwater catchment can be for reuse of the water or, more typically, it can be caught for infiltration purposes. Alternate water supplies such as cooling tower bleed-off water, air conditioning condensate, and greywater can and typically are reused for non-potable uses that include landscape irrigation and toilet flushing. While rainwater collection is the main emphasis of this book, the collection and use or reuse of all of these supplies are recommended for applicability to a new or existing project.

Acknowledgments

IT IS TIME THAT WE TAKE our futures and our children's futures seriously and start providing solutions today for tomorrow's world. One specific and very serious issue is fresh-water supplies. It is out of this desperate need for understanding and examples of how we can extend our current resources for future generations that this book has been assembled.

Thank you to all project owners, designers, and builders that have taken a chance to try something new and innovative in the quest to conserve water for my child and yours.

Thank you, Victoria, for your graphic support and keeping the standards high.

1 Introduction to Rainwater Harvesting

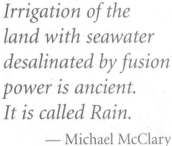

*Irrigation of the
land with seawater
desalinated by fusion
power is ancient.
It is called Rain.*

— Michael McClary

IN MARCH OF 2005 the Millennium Ecosystem Assessment (MEA) was released. This report, requested by United Nations Secretary-General Kofi Annan in 2000, is titled *Living Beyond Our Means: Natural Assets and Human Well-Being*. The report is a culmination of the findings of 1,360 experts from across the world. Their findings focus on the condition and trends of the ecosystems, scenarios for the future, possible responses, and assessments at a sub-global level. The main message presented by this group is one of warning, stating that human activity is putting an incredible strain on the natural functions of the Earth, one that we can no longer ignore. The team of experts argues that we must learn to recognize the true value of nature and the protection of these natural assets can no longer be seen as an option.

Spring rain clouds

HEATHER KINKADE-LEVARIO

Feather and Fur Animal Hospital rainwater tank, Austin, TX

Freshwater is one natural asset listed as a priority.[1]

People use a lot of water for drinking, cooking, washing, and irrigating landscapes. They use even more water to produce food, material products, manufactured items such as clothing, and to run buildings. The total amount of freshwater consumed by an individual, business, or nation to produce goods and services is known as the water footprint of that individual, business, or nation.[2] In an effort to reduce our collective freshwater footprint, this book presents options for water supplies beyond groundwater and surface water that help to reduce the amount of these water types

withdrawn and purified for use by humans. There are many types of water included in the following definitions:

- Atmospheric water – Rain and fog.

- Blue water – Water from aquifers, rivers, and lakes.[3]

- Green water – Soil moisture.[4]

- Stormwater – Rainwater that has hit the ground.

- Greywater (Graywater) – Wastewater from a laundry, bathtub, shower, and/or a bath sink.[5]

- Alternate water – Water that has been used previously, typically by equipment, including cooling tower bleed-

*Passive rainwater harvesting:
Island Wood School, Seattle, WA*

*HEB store displays rainwater
tanks at their entry road, Austin, TX*

off water, air-conditioning condensate, and water used in labs to cool equipment.

- Black water – Water from toilets and kitchen sinks.

- Reclaim water – Water that has gone through a sewer treatment process and has been filtered and processed for reuse in various ways, including large scale irrigation.

We need to change the way we use our freshwater and need to look at our designs that involve water to use what we have as efficiently as possible. Therefore, we must "design for water." While the main focus of this book is on rainwater

Reunion Building with two 4,400-gallon rainwater tanks

collection for potable and non-potable use, the case studies presented will discuss water collection for infiltration and increasing green water, fog collection, stormwater catchment, and alternate water reuse—including greywater reuse. The case studies presented will demonstrate that freshwater—blue water—does not have to be the first choice for a water source, which means we can reduce our water footprint.

United States Green Building Council (USGBC) Leadership in Energy and Environmental Design (LEED)

Many of the projects presented in this document have attained a specific green building level of LEED Certification. The designation of Certification, Silver, Gold, or Platinum means that the project has met all the criteria set by USGBC for these various LEED levels. The

USGBC Preamble released May 25, 2006 states the following:

"Whereas USGBC is dedicated to improving conditions for humanity and nature, honoring and enhancing the prospects for both through the creation of a built environment that is mutually beneficial, we hereby acknowledge our allegiance to the essential values:

Sustainability: Respect the limits of natural systems and non-renewable resources by seeking solutions that produce an abundance of natural and social capital;

Equity: Respect all communities and cultures and aspire to an equal socio-economic opportunity for all;

Inclusiveness: Practice and promote openness, broad participation, and full consideration of consequence

Passive rainwater harvesting: Pima Community College F Plaza gutter drops to splash pad of rocks next to a tree

Passive rainwater harvesting: Pima Community College swale next to sidewalk collects storm-water runoff for vegetation

in all aspects of decision-making processes;

Progress: Strive for immediate and measurable indicators of environmental, social, and economic prosperity;

Connectedness: Recognize the critical linkage between humanity and nature as well as the importance of place-based decision-making to effective stewardship."

The more the points met by the buildings, the higher the level up to the maximum points for a Platinum rating. More can be found on this subject at www.usgbc.org.

Istanbul, TK cistern sign

Inside the Istanbul cistern

Rainwater Catchment History

Many cultures throughout the world have used captured rainwater. The Middle East, Asia, ancient Rome, and Mexico utilized rainwater harvesting. In India, simple stone-rubble structures for capturing rainwater date back to 3000 BC.[6] A civilization as early as 2000 BC survived in the Negev Desert of what is now Israel by storing hillside runoff in cisterns.[7]

A historical document of the time mentions water cisterns and the habit of having at least one rainwater-collecting cistern per home that would range in size from 35 to 200 cubic meters. These residential cisterns were

Ancient Roman aqueduct

typically below ground and were pear or bottle shaped.[8] The first community cisterns ranged in size from 4,000 cubic meters to large reservoirs such as the one found in Madaba that could hold 42,750 cubic meters. These cisterns were technologically sophisticated with sediment traps or "first-flush" systems to catch sediment, mud, and sand prior to allowing the water to enter the cistern.[9] Huge rock hewn cisterns and canals can be found in Petra. In all of these locations, rainwater was typically collected off rooftops and plazas.

In Rome, rainwater was collected from the covered walkways and diverted to small pools located in gardens for esthetic purposes and for future use as irrigation water.[10] The Romans designed villas and entire cities to take advantage of collected rainwater and they used the water as the primary source for drinking and other domestic uses.[11]

Underground cisterns in central Mexico stored collected rainwater from plazas and rooftops for human consumption and irrigation.[12] In the Yucatan Peninsula, archaeological remains from AD 300 indicate ground catchment systems known as Chultuns were used to collect rainwater.[13] In the United States and Canada, rainwater collection systems have historically been used by native inhabitants and settlers in isolated areas where there were no existing municipal water supplies. In many areas they are still used, as demonstrated by a 1995 survey, which concluded that in that year there were roughly 250,000 rainwater harvesting systems in use in the United States.[14] Rainwater harvesting systems are currently gaining popularity as many communities promote sustainable development.

Mexican home with a corrugated metal cistern next to the house, used for vegetables in the front yard

Belize rainwater tank at the end of a driveway

Hawaiian rainwater tank

Throughout this book, you will notice that volumes, weights, costs, and other measures are referenced. Unless otherwise noted, these are presented in standard US measure. There is a metric conversion table in an Appendix at the end of the book for most measurement conversions.

2 A Rainwater Harvesting System

> *Arguments over water are resolved by rain.*
>
> — Japanese proverb

RAIN, A FORM of precipitation, is the first form of water in the hydrologic cycle, the continuous circulation of water in the earth-atmosphere system. Rain is the primary source of water that feeds rivers, lakes, and groundwater aquifers. Rivers, lakes, and groundwater are all secondary sources of water. Currently, most of us depend entirely on secondary sources for our water supplies. The value of rainwater, the primary source of water, is typically ignored. Rainwater catchment directly responds to the value of this primary source of water, making optimal use of rainwater where it falls.

Rainwater collection has been used for several thousand years as a way to take advantage of seasonal precipitation that would otherwise be lost to runoff or evaporation. While rainwater can provide water for many uses, the most common

Heather Kinkade-Levario

Heather Kinkade-Levario

LEFT:
Rain scupper on a commercial building
RIGHT:
Corrugated metal pipe cistern located within a walled residential patio

Rooftop catchment

use is for agricultural irrigation and residential potable water. Most applied definitions of rainwater collection, or rainwater harvesting as it is typically referred to, detail numerous methods for collecting, storing, and conserving runoff from an assortment of sources for unlimited purposes in arid and semi-arid regions.[15]

One definition of rainwater harvesting states that the word "harvesting" refers to a process that first requires a method of "seeding" the clouds to induce the rain.[16] For the purposes of this book the word harvesting will refer to the collection of rain without an artificial inducement. The aim of rainwater harvesting is to concentrate runoff and collect it in a basin or cistern to be stored for future use.

Rainwater captured from roof catchments is the easiest and most common method used to harvest rainwater. It is, however, not the only harvesting method. Rainwater may be collected from any hard surface, such as stone or concrete patios, and asphalt parking lots. Typically, once the rain hits the ground it is no longer referred to as rain, but as stormwater. Landscapes can also be contoured to retain the stormwater runoff.

There are numerous identified benefits of water catchment from either rooftop or ground level:

- It provides a self-sufficient water supply located close to the user.

- It reduces the need for, and hence the cost of, pumping groundwater.

- It provides high-quality soft water that is low in mineral content.

- It augments the supply and improves the quality of groundwater when it reaches the aquifer after it has been applied to the landscape or crops.

- It reduces and may even eliminate soil salts as it dissolves and moves the salts down through the soil.
- It mitigates urban flooding and, as a result, reduces soil erosion in urban areas.
- Rooftop rainwater harvesting is usually less expensive than other water sources.
- Rooftop rainwater harvesting systems are easy to construct, operate, and maintain.
- In coastal areas where salt water intrusion into the aquifer is a problem, rainwater provides good quality water, and when recharged to groundwater, reduces groundwater salinity while helping to maintain a balance between the fresh and saline water interface.
- On islands with limited fresh-water aquifers, rainwater harvesting is the preferred source of water for domestic use.
- Occasionally, there are economic advantages such as rebates from municipalities for a reduction in use and dependency on municipal water.

Rainwater harvesting and stormwater catchment consists of up to six primary components depending on the degree of water quality required. These components include catchment, conveyance, filtration, storage, distribution, and purification, all of which are defined in the next few pages. The amount of water collected depends on catchment size, surface texture, surface porosity, and slope conditions. Regardless of the catchment surface material, a loss of from 10 to 70 percent may be expected due to runoff material absorption or percolation, evaporation, and inefficiencies in the collection process.

There are numerous ways to connect the catchment areas to the desired point of use or to a landscape holding area. A landscape holding area, essentially a passive stormwater distribution system, is an earth basin that is used to irrigate plants through an overland flow system: water infiltrates through the soil and is then conserved in a plant's root zone—green water—for its consumptive use. Distribution systems that direct rainwater and stormwater runoff can be as simple as landscape swales, sloped sidewalks, and concrete street gutters, or they can be sophisticated systems such as roof gutters and downspouts, collection and distribution systems for sub-asphalt collection, filters and a cistern to delay or control distribution of rainwater runoff, perforated pipes and drip irrigation, or pumps to move and treatment systems to purify the collected water.

Downspout and gutter on a residential roof

HEATHER KINKADE-LEVARIO

Components of a System

Whether it is large or small, a rainwater harvesting system has six basic components:

1. Catchment area: the surface upon which the rain falls. It may be a roof or impervious pavement and may include landscaped areas.

2. Conveyance: channels or pipes that transport the water from catchment area to storage.

3. Roof washing: the systems that filter and remove contaminants and debris. This includes first-flush devices.

4. Storage: cisterns or tanks where collected rainwater is stored.

5. Distribution: the system that delivers the rainwater, either by gravity or pump.

6. Purification: includes filtering equipment, distillation, and additives to settle, filter, and disinfect the collected rainwater.

Purification is only required for potable systems and would typically occur prior to distribution. Details 2.1 and 2.2 illustrate a nonpotable process for commercial and residential applications.

Catchment Area

A catchment area is the defined surface area, typically a rooftop, upon which rainwater falls and is eventually collected. Rainwater harvesting for nonpotable use can be accomplished with any type of roofing material. For potable use, the best roof materials are metal, clay, and concrete. Water for drinking purposes should not be collected from roofs containing zinc coatings, copper, asbestos sheets, or asphaltic compounds. Roofs with lead flashings or painted with lead-based paints should not be used. An acceptable roofing material for systems that will be catching water intended for human consumption is Raincoat 2000. It is a three-part roof coating product for flat or semi-flat roofs that is approved by the National Sanitation Foundation (NSF) for potable water harvesting.

Although rooftops are the typical catchment area, patio surfaces, driveways, parking lots, or channeled gullies can also serve as catchment areas. However, because of the higher risk of contamination, stormwater collected from ground-level catchment areas should not be used for potable purposes unless a purification system accompanies the distribution system.

Rainbarn is a term describing an open-air shed or ramada designed with a large roof area, the sole purpose of which is to catch rainwater. The structure's large roof area could also provide shelter for a variety of uses—a patio, carport, hay

Flat rooftop catchment area finished with Raincoat 2000

Tim Pope

storage, or farm equipment storage—thereby serving multiple functions. Typically, a cistern is housed under a rainbarn.[17] Rainwater is slightly acidic, which means it will dissolve and carry minerals into the storage system from any catchment surface. When a system is intended for potable water collection, the first step should be to test the water collected from the proposed catchment surface to determine its content and what items need to be removed by a filtration system or if the catchment surface needs to be altered.

The total amount of water that is received in the form of rainfall over an area is called the rainwater endowment of that area. The actual amount of rainwater that can be effectively harvested from the rainwater endowment is called the rainwater harvesting potential.[18] Rainwater yields vary with the size and texture of the catchment area. A maximum of 90 percent of a rainfall can be effectively captured through

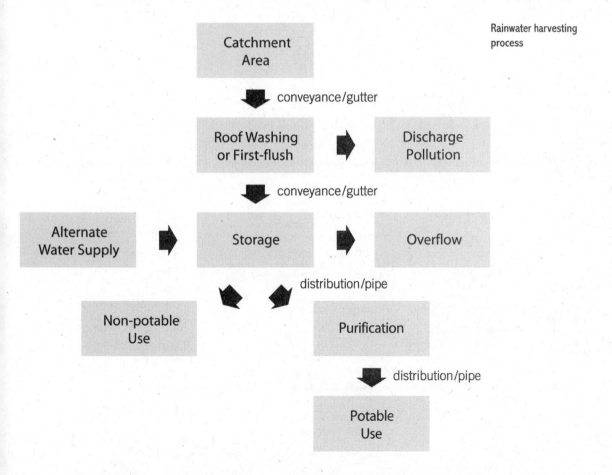

Rainwater harvesting process

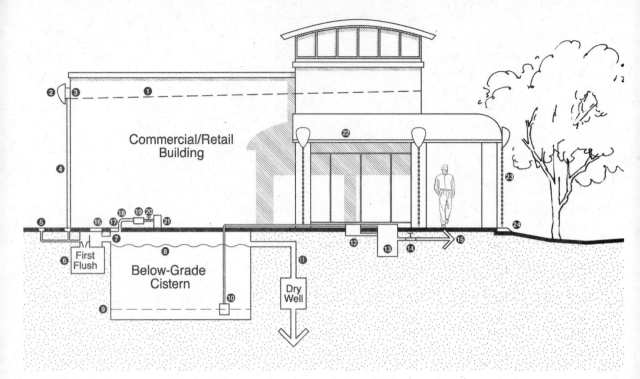

Detail 2.1

Typical components of a commercial/industrial building rainwater harvesting

NOTE: Cistern size and catchment area should be balanced for maximum accumulated storage. Not all site rainfall should be directed to cistern, only the quantity required to maintain the proposed landscape irrigation budget.

1. Single-plane or double-plane butterfly rooftop collection.

2. Optional decorative scupper cover.

3. Scupper to downspout.

4. Downspout sized per local plumbing code, sediment trap at ground level.

5. Catchbasin for paved/hard surface ground level runoff collection, with sediment trap.

6. Debris, sediment, and oil interceptor.

7. Rainwater inlet. Inlet to cistern must be a minimum of 10 inches below top of cistern. An inflow smoothing filter may be appropriate at this location depending on proximity of rainwater inlet to irrigation supply filter. The smoothing filter will slow rainwater inlet turbulence that may disturb the fine sediment settled on the bottom of the cistern.

8. Maximum water level to be 12 inches below top of cistern.

9. Minimal level of water to maintain priming in landscape irrigation pump (approximately 12 inches), level of water to be determined by engineer or irrigation specialist.

10. Landscape irrigation supply filter with automatic shutoff to maintain priming in pump if water falls below minimum level in cistern. Locate filter a minimum of 6 inches from cistern bottom to avoid settled fine sediment.

11. Cistern overflow (same size as inlet) to a dry well or gravity outlet to landscape basin if site conditions allow. An additional option would be to outlet to an adjacent flood retention underground storage pipe that is tied to a dry well. Cistern overflow must be a minimum of 12 inches below top of cistern to avoid contamination of alternate water supply (if proposed).

12. Sand filter (optional).

13. Landscape irrigation pump and pressure tank.

14. Typical valve.

15. Water supply line for irrigation system.

16. Thirty-two inch access for cleaning.

17. Twenty-four inch access for cleaning.

18. Alternate water supply, must not obstruct the 24-inch access. Alternate water supply may be proposed for a cistern manual fill option for droughts and plant establishment periods when additional water is required. Alternate water supply may also be automatic for fill option when rainwater supplies are inefficient.

19. Atmospheric vacuum breaker.

20. Typical valve.

21. Alternate water source, possibly domestic or municipal supply.

22. Gutter with leaf screen if building is adjacent to trees.

23. Rainchains or downspouts to splash pads and depressed landscape areas.

24. Splash pad.

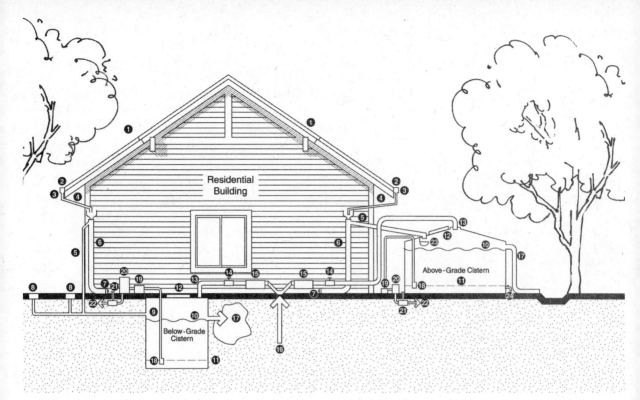

Detail 2.2

Typical components of a residential building rainwater harvesting system for landscape irrigation

NOTE: Both above-grade and below-grade cisterns are shown. For residential systems, either may be appropriate. It is not necessary to have both types of systems. Cistern size and catchment area should be balanced for maximum accumulated storage. Not all site rainfall runoff needs to be directed to cistern, only the quantity required to maintain the proposed landscape irrigation budget.

1. Rooftop collection.

2. Gutter with leaf screen if building is adjacent to trees.

3. Five- to six-inch gutters, sized per local plumbing code.

4. Downspout sized per local plumbing code, sediment trap for ground-level catchment or direct to cistern.

5. Pipe to cistern, typically 4-inch diameter schedule 40 PVC pipe.

6. Debris and sediment interceptor, first-flush device.

7. Screw-off end cap for cleaning.

8. Catchbasin for paved/hard surface ground-level runoff collection, with sediment trap.

9. Rainwater inlet, inlet to cistern must be a minimum of 10 inches below top of cistern. An inflow smoothing filter may be appropriate at this location depending on proximity of rainwater inlet to irrigation supply filter. The smoothing filter will slow rainwater inlet turbulence that may disturb the fine sediment settled on the bottom of the cistern.

10. Maximum water level to be 12 inches below top of cistern.

11. Minimal level of water to maintain priming in landscape irrigation pump (approximately 12 inches), level of water to be determined by engineer or irrigation specialist.

12. Twenty-four inch access for cleaning.

13. Alternate water supply, must not obstruct the 24-inch access. Alternate water supply may be proposed for a cistern manual-fill option for droughts and plant establishment periods when additional water is required. Alternate water supply may also be automatic for fill option when rainwater supplies are inefficient.

14. Typical valve.

15. Atmospheric vacuum breaker.

16. Alternate water source, possibly domestic or municipal supply.

17. Cistern overflow (same size as inlet) to a dry well or gravity outlet to landscape basin if site conditions allow. An additional option would be to outlet to an adjacent flood retention underground storage pipe that is tied to a dry well. Cistern overflow must be a minimum of 12 inches below top of cistern to avoid contamination of alternate water supply, or be 6 inches below any debris strainers in an above-grade cistern.

18. Landscape irrigation supply filter with automatic shutoff to maintain priming in pump if water falls below minimum level in cistern. Locate filter a minimum of 6 inches from cistern bottom to avoid settled fine sediment.

19. Optional sand filter.

20. Landscape irrigation pump and pressure tank.

21. Typical valve.

22. Water supply line for irrigation system.

23. Removable leaf and debris strainer basket.

24. Hose bib for draining cistern.

rooftop rainwater harvesting. The quality of the captured rainwater depends, in part, upon catchment texture: the best water quality comes from the smoother, more impervious catchment or roofing materials.

Captured rainwater quality is also determined by rainfall pattern and frequency. Both the greater the storm event, i.e., the rainfall extent and the quantity of rain that falls, and the shorter the time between storms influence the cleanliness of the catchment area. Greater rainwater volumes and frequencies will transport fewer pollutants to the first-flush device (described below in the Roof Washing section) or the storage unit.

Conveyance

A commonly used rainwater conveyance system is comprised of gutters with downspouts and/or rainchains. Gutters and downspouts direct rain from rooftop catchment surfaces to cisterns or storage tanks. Rainchains are lengths of chain that hang from gutters and direct rainwater down their lengths, thereby minimizing splash. In the rainwater harvesting process, they may be used when water is being collected for below-grade storage or directed to a landscaped area.

Gutters and downspouts can be easily obtained as standard household construction materi-

als, or they can be specifically designed to enhance a building façade and maximize the amount of harvested rainfall. The materials for gutters and downspouts range from vinyl and galvanized steel to aluminum, copper, and stainless steel. Gutters should typically be square, rectangular, or half round in shape and, at a minimum, 5 or 6 inches wide. They should have an outer edge higher than the roof-side edge, have splash guards at roof valleys, slope towards downspouts at one-sixteenth to one-quarter inch per 10-foot length of gutter, and be installed per manufacturer's guidelines for hangers and connection points (approximately one bracket every 30 inches).

A typical connection material from a downspout to a cistern is a 3- or 4-inch diameter schedule 40 PVC pipe or the more environmentally sensitive ABS pipe. For potable rainwater collection, only schedule 40 PVC should be used, as it is the only PVC made from "virgin" material—i.e., material made from new material, not recycled material that may have picked up contaminants from its previous use. Coated aluminum downspouts are acceptable for potable collections. No ABS, DWV PVC, copper, lead-containing, or galvanized pipes should be used for potable collections. Downspouts

Gutter and downspout on a residential building

Gutter and downspout attached to cistern

should be placed as appropriate to allow 1 square inch of outlet (downspout) space for every 100 square feet of roof area to be drained. As an example, a 4-inch diameter downspout can drain approximately 400 square feet of roof area.

There are two types of conveyance systems, wet and dry. A wet system involves downspouts that lead to a storage system where standing water is maintained; downspouts run down the wall and underground and then up into the tank. In a dry system, the downspouts drain down into the storage system, thus eliminating any standing water in the conveyance system after a rain event. Dry systems reduce the potential of mosquito habitat and are the type of systems detailed in this book.

Gutters should be kept clean and debris-free to maintain the longevity of the gutter material —clean gutters dry out after a rain faster and dry gutters last up to three times longer than wet gutters, which equates to a significant cost savings. The Uniform Plumbing Code has an appendix dedicated to rainwater systems, with guidelines to size gutters, downspouts, and lateral pipes. The applicable plumbing code should be reviewed for any design of rainwater conveyance systems.

To keep leaves and other debris from entering a rooftop rainwater harvesting system, the gutters should have continuous leaf screens made out of one-quarter-inch wire mesh screen in a metal frame or an equally efficient product covering the

HEATHER KINKADE-LEVARIO

Mobile trailer under a rainbarn that is attached to a cistern

Rainbarns used for rainwater collection systems

HEATHER KINKADE-LEVARIO

LEFT:
Rainchain used by a commercial building to direct rainwater to the landscape
RIGHT:
Rainchain splash pad

Specifications on a plastic tank

entire length of gutter. Installing leaf screens will help reduce a rainwater harvesting system's maintenance, eliminate flammable material from the roof area, reduce mosquito breeding habitat, and eliminate the need for frequent and potentially hazardous use of a ladder to clean the gutters.

Roof Washing

Roof washing is the initial process in reducing the debris and soluble pollutants that may enter a rainwater harvesting system. Roof-washing systems may use one or several components to filter or collect debris and soluble pollutants, including gutter leaf guards, rainheads, screens, and/

Empty tanks under a wooden deck ready for installation

A 240-gallon collection tank from which collected rainwater is pumped to a remote storage tank

At-grade concrete cistern

or first-flush devices (described later). Use of the first three of these allows the maximum amount of rainwater that encounters the filtering unit to be harvested while removing debris. Use of first-flush devices is important when rainwater is collected without the use of gutter leaf guards, leafslides, or rain-

heads, or if the rainwater is to be used for human consumption.

Roofs, like other large, exposed areas, continuously receive deposits of debris, leaves, silt, and pollutants on their surface. All rainwater dislodges and carries away some of these deposits, but, during any given rainfall, the stormwater that falls first

SANDY MURDOCH, RAIN HARVESTING PTY LTD

Blue Mountain Mesh
all-steel gutter mesh covering
a gutter on a tile roof

Roof washer on display for
purchase at a rainwater harvesting systems supply company

HEATHER KINKADE-LEVARIO

carries the highest concentration of debris and soluble pollutants. First-flush devices collect and dispose of this initial rain before it contaminates previously harvested and stored rainwater.

Terry Thomas, a specialist in rooftop rainwater harvesting, is the Director of the Development Technology Unit at the School of Engineering at the University of Warwick in England. He has identified several reasons for reducing debris and silt that may enter a rainwater storage system, including:

- Reduction of frequency of tank cleaning

- Reduction of bacterial inflow that is often attached to solids

- Reduction in the nutrient levels in cisterns/tanks that, in turn, reduces or even eliminates mosquito larvae growth

- Reduction in organic loading, creating less of a chance of

anaerobic conditions and odor in the cistern/tank

Roof-washing systems provide a means of accomplishing these objectives. The simplest roof-washing system is a first-flush device that consists of a standpipe, the container for collecting the initial rainwater runoff, and a gutter downspout located prior to the cistern or storage tank inlet. Because a typical standpipe does not automatically outlet to a storm drain, a screw-on cleanout plug should be located at the end of the standpipe. The standpipe should be emptied after each rain event to prepare for future use and to eliminate the standing water from becoming foul and stagnant due to its content of debris and soluble pollutants, and thereby contaminating future collected rainwater.

A German company has developed a simple and self-cleaning filter—called a WISY filter—that combines the standpipe/downspout components of a roof-washing system. This system does not flush the first gallons of collected rainwater as does a typical standpipe, which, if the rainwater is proposed for potable use, may mean more purification will be required before the stored rainwater is used for human consumption. Instead, the WISY filter, with its interior lining of fine mesh, diverts up to 90 percent of the rainwater from the enhanced standpipe to the storage tank/cistern while allowing the remainder to pass on through, carrying the unwanted leaves, debris, and silt into the storm drain or an adjacent landscape.

Capacities of first-flush devices may vary depending on the catchment size and ultimate use of the rainwater. Rainwater collected from a rooftop will typically be cleaner than stormwater collected from a surface or pavement area, which means the storage capacity of the first-flush device does not need to be large. Stormwater collected from surface or pavement areas may require longer settling periods for suspended solids and an absorbent pillow to remove oil and grease; therefore, a more sophisticated and larger capacity first-flush device is required.

A first-flush device for small rooftops (less than 1,000 square feet) should provide storage capacity for diversion of the first 5 gallons of collected rainwater. Larger rooftops should provide a container for diversion of the initial 10 gallons of rainfall per 1,000 square feet of roof area. With very large rooftops or paved catchment areas (one acre or more), a maximum of 500 (or 1,000 if collected from dirty pavement) gallons for each rain event should be collected and disposed of in a first-flush device. Some residential roof washers are self-cleaning and adjust to the amount of rain received or the rate at which the

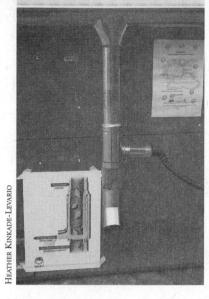

WISY filter display: black pipe leads to cistern

Detail of WISY filter

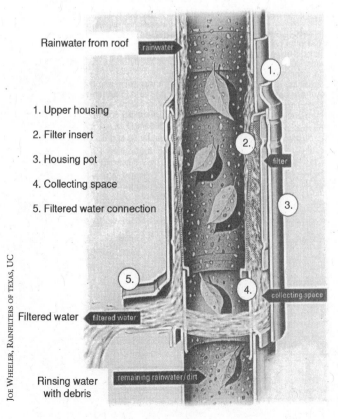

Rainwater from roof — rainwater

1. Upper housing

2. Filter insert

3. Housing pot

4. Collecting space

5. Filtered water connection

1.

2. filter

3.

5.

4. collecting space

Filtered water — filtered water

Rinsing water with debris — remaining rainwater/dirt

German product display:
rainhead filter

German product display:
cistern overflow attached
to inlet filter

German product display:
cistern inlet filter

rainwater enters the roof washing device.

Use of a first-flush device is especially important when a rain event follows a long period of no rain, since, during dry spells, debris and other pollutants build up on catchment surfaces. In this case, a large volume of water may be required to remove the catchment surface contaminants, possibly surpassing the volume allowed in a specified first-flush device. This means some contaminants will not be diverted and will be allowed to enter the rainwater storage system. When a second rain event closely follows one that was strong enough to sufficiently wash the catchment area, use of the first-flush device during the second rain event may not be required.

However, if the first rain event was not strong enough to move the catchment area contaminants, diversion of the second rain event's initial rainwater runoff to the first-flush device may be warranted, particularly if it is potable water that is to be protected from contaminants. Where potable water is not the issue, a second first-flush may only waste valuable rainwater. Instead, collection in the cistern may be warranted, especially for non-potable uses such as landscape irrigation, laundry, toilet flushing, etc. Some first-flush devices such as the SafeRain will reset and fill faster with a second close rain event, thereby wasting less rainwater from an already clean roof.

A roof-washing system generally produces the best results when combined with the use of filtering devices on gutters, downspouts, and first-flush devices. This is especially true when potable water is the desired end product. The most common filtering devices are gutter leaf screens, which filter large leaves and other debris. However, because leaf screens are not designed to filter smaller matter, water released from the gutters will often contain fine debris or even dissolved contaminants.

Fortunately, the filtering process can be augmented by use

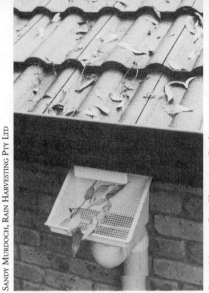

SANDY MURDOCH, RAIN HARVESTING PTY LTD

SANDY MURDOCH, RAIN HARVESTING PTY LTD

LEFT:
*Leaf Eater downspout filter
(or rainhead) mounted in the
traditional way at the gutter.*
RIGHT:
*Leaf Eater downspout
filter (or rainhead) mid
mounted on wall*

of a downspout that incorporates a self-cleaning system called a rainhead. A rainhead is a square funnel topped by a screen set at an angle of about 33 degrees to the lower horizontal edge of the funnel. As the water washes over the angled screen, the debris is forced toward the screen's lower edge and away from the building, while the rainwater continues through the funnel screen.

Rainheads can be used with either a dry or a wet rainwater conveyance system. For use with a wet system, an Australian company has designed the Leaf Beater system, which provides a second horizontal screen that prevents mosquitoes from entering the conveyance system and reaching the storage tank/cistern. A Leafslide box may also be used. The box works in the same manner as the rainhead by allowing the rainwater's vertical drop to clean the filter. The Leafslide achieves best results when two

sections of the guttering system are diverted simultaneously through the box. As noted, the combining of filtering methods such as gutter leaf screens, leaf-slides, rainheads, and first-flush devices is desirable when the harvested rainwater is intended for human consumption. When the collected rainwater is to be used solely for landscape irrigation, only the large debris may need to be filtered, as some items, such as bird droppings, may be beneficial to the plants receiving the rainwater.

Storage

Most of the components of a rooftop rainwater harvesting system are assumed costs in a building project. For example, all buildings have a roof and, typically, gutters and downspouts. Most homes and businesses also have landscape materials and irrigation systems placed around the structures. The cisterns or

LEFT:
Small cistern next to rooftop catchment with no first-flush
RIGHT:
Metal cistern attached to a downspout

Cisterns of various sizes and colors

storage tanks represent the largest investment in a rainwater harvesting system because most homes and businesses are not initially fitted with a storage system. Storage cisterns can be divided into three classes:

- Surface, at-grade or above-ground cisterns

- Below-grade, underground (including partially underground) tanks

- Integral cisterns or tanks built into a dwelling or commercial building

Most cisterns and tanks have three distinct components, all of which need to be waterproof:

the base, the sides, and the cover. They also contain several minor components as shown in Details 2.1 and 2.2: water inlet, water outlet, access hatch, and means of draining. A typical storage cistern is covered and made of stone, steel, concrete, ferro-cement, plastic, or fiberglass. A storage system should be durable, attractive, watertight, clean, smooth inside, sealed with a non-toxic joint sealant, easy to operate, and able to withstand the forces of standing water. A tight cover is essential to prevent evaporation and mosquito breeding, and to keep insects, birds, lizards, frogs, and rodents from entering the tank. Cisterns and tanks should not allow sunlight to enter or algae will grow inside the container.

Some storage tanks contain settling compartments that encourage any roof or pavement runoff contaminants to settle rather than remain suspended. Storage tanks can have an inlet from a sand filter or directly from the gutters through a leaf and debris filter. They must also have an overflow equal in size to the inlet volume and an outlet or drain. The overflow should daylight to a landscape basin or an adjacent drainage system.

The outlet leads to the distribution system. Some systems, especially if they are a sole source of water or if landscape irrigation requires supplemental water, may have an inlet pipe from an alternate, make-up water source such as a municipal water supply. Whenever an alternate, make-up water source is used with a storage system, an

HEATHER KINKADE-LEVARIO

White tanks, usually placed in dark locations to eliminate exposure to light

HEATHER KINKADE-LEVARIO

HEATHER KINKADE-LEVARIO

LEFT:
Corrugated metal pipe cisterns, 5 feet in diameter by 10 feet in height, 1,468 gallons each
RIGHT:
Larger cistern holding 7,000 gallons of rainwater

German product display: section removed from a cistern to show a floating intake

German product display: cistern side cut away to show an inlet flow calming device

air gap must be maintained between the high water line or highest flood line in the storage cistern/tank and the inlet of the alternate water. A typical air gap is 14 inches. The overflow line should be placed to maintain the maximum high water line in the cistern/tank. An additional security to avoid contamination of the alternate water supply is a backflow valve, which should be installed in the alternate water line prior to the water reaching the storage container.

The type of storage system chosen by a prospective rainwater harvester depends on several technical and economic considerations:

- Options available locally
- Space available
- Storage quantity desired
- Cost of the vessel
- Cost of excavation and soil composition (sand, clay, loam, or rock)
- Aesthetics (possibility of integrating cistern into the building)

Answers to the above considerations will help to determine if an above-ground cistern or below-grade tank will be used. The above-ground storage system can be easily purchased off the shelf in most communities, allowing for easy inspection and gravity water extraction/draining. The above-ground storage systems require space, can be

more expensive, and are susceptible to damage from constant exposure to the elements. Below-grade storage systems generally are reasonably priced, require little or no above-ground space, are unobtrusive, and permit thinner cistern walls due to the support of the surrounding ground. Extracting water from below-grade systems is more difficult—often requiring a pump—and leaks and failures are more difficult to detect. In addition, tree roots or overhead traffic may damage the below-grade storage system.

Water in a storage cistern will typically consist of three layers.[19] The top layer, the aerobic zone, will be fully aged water; the middle layer will be ageing water; and the bottom layer, the anaerobic zone, will be a mixing water that contains the most solids. To take advantage of this stratification, especially for potable systems, a floating pump intake that avoids the surface film where floating particles may be present would best allow the use of the fully aged storage cistern water.

The best system would have two intakes, one floating intake for potable uses and one stationary intake lower in the tank to allow the mixing water to be used for nonpotable uses. The best overflow would be one that would allow water to exit from the anaerobic zone in the tank. Even better would be an overflow that would vacuum or suction out the sludge that may accumulate in the bottom of a tank or cistern.

A cistern that is cool and devoid of sunlight allows water quality to increase with time. When photosynthesis cannot take place, most organisms die off as their food source is eliminated. With each rain event a new supply of sediment and organisms will enter the storage unit. The sediment, while not usually unhealthy, can initially discolor and flavor the water, but will ultimately settle to the bottom of the storage container. It is best to remove water from a cistern or tank at a position that is farthest from a runoff inlet to allow the water time to age before it is used. Some storage containers may require baffles, inflow smoothing filters, or turbulent dissipaters to slow the inlet turbulence that remixes the ageing water. In cisterns that are open to the air and allow mosquito growth, a Bacillus thuringienis-israelensis (Bt-i) Mosquito Dunk disk can be used to eliminate mosquito growth.

Proper foundations are very important for all types of cisterns: water is very heavy (a 500-gallon tank full of water will weigh more than two tons)[20] and soil settling may occur and damage a tank. Manholes or access hatches should be included in buried cisterns for cleaning and inspection. Some systems may have a back-up cistern or tank. While this is an additional cost, it permits servicing of one unit without losing the operation of the entire system. Storage systems should be located to maximize efficiency of both supply and demand points as well as to use gravity where possible.

Distribution

Stored rainwater may be conveyed or distributed by gravity or by pumping. If a tank is located uphill or above the area proposed for irrigation, gravity may work. Most plumbing fixtures, appliances, and drip irrigation systems require at least 20 pounds per square inch (psi) for proper operation. Standard municipal water supply pressures are typically in the 40 psi to 80 psi range.[21] As a general rule, water gains 1.0 pound per square inch of pressure for every 2.31 feet of rise or lift. Pumps, rather than elevated tanks, are typically used to extract both below-grade and at-grade cistern- or tank-stored water. Submersible or at-grade pumps may be used in any rainwater storage system. Self-priming pumps with floating filter intakes and automatic shutoffs—for times when water levels are insufficient—are optimal equipment. As mentioned previously, the bottom few inches of stored water will typically contain very fine settled sediment

HEATHER KINKADE-LEVARIO

Bacillus thuringienis-israelensis (Bt-i) Mosquito Dunk

Metal tank base ring

HEATHER KINKADE-LEVARIO

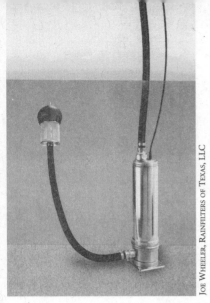

Submersible pump and floating filter intake

JOE WHEELER, RAINFILTERS OF TEXAS, LLC

LEFT:
100mm Vented Flap Valve and /or tank overflow outlet.
RIGHT:
The 50mm Flap Valve incorporates a non-corrosive plastic screen of 0.955mm and the 100mm Flap Valve utilizes a rust-proof stainless steel screen of 0.955mm; both are vermin-proof

and should be avoided if possible. Depending on the proximity of the rainwater inlet and pump intake, as well as the time rainwater is left to settle or calm, the pumping process may need to be delayed for a short duration after a rain event.

The storage system overflow may act as a distribution system that delivers excess water to an adjacent landscape. All overflows exposed or outletting above ground should have some means of stopping rodents and insects from entering the storage system. Fine screens may be placed over the end of pipes and, in areas of high rain quantities, water traps—similar to sinks and toilets—may be used.

For landscape irrigation, stored rainwater may go through additional filters before it is directed into an irrigation pump and distribution lines. This may be necessary to avoid clogging the irrigation system. For a potable water system, the water must go through a purification process prior to distribution.

Purification

If harvested rainwater is to be used for potable supplies, the rainwater would be pumped from the cistern to the purification system and then distributed to the points of use such as a kitchen sink faucet. In a non-potable system no purification process is required. Potable water treatment systems normally include filters, disinfection, and buffering for pH control. Filtration can include any of the following: in-line or multi-cartridge, activated charcoal, reverse osmosis, nano-filtration, mixed media, or slow sand. Disinfecting can include boiling or distilling, chemical treatments, ultraviolet lights, and/or ozonization. Rainwater intended for human consumption should undergo several steps, including screening, settling, filtering, and disinfecting. Filtering and disinfecting are two components of rainwater harvesting that will enhance a potable system.

When water is being used from storage, sediment filtration should be a maximum of 5-micron, followed by a 0.5-micron carbon filter or an equivalent 1-micron absolute filter. These ultra filters should be approved by the National Sanitation Foundation for cyst removal. These filters will remove Giaradia and Cryptosporidium from the water supply. The ultraviolet disinfections are perfect

SANDY MURDOCH, RAIN HARVESTING PTY LTD

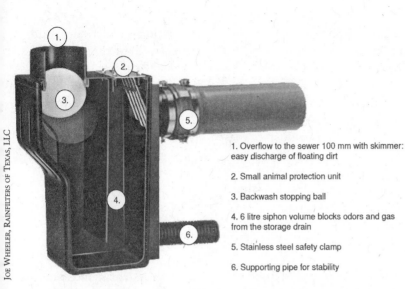

JOE WHEELER, RAINFILTERS OF TEXAS, LLC

1. Overflow to the sewer 100 mm with skimmer: easy discharge of floating dirt

2. Small animal protection unit

3. Backwash stopping ball

4. 6 litre siphon volume blocks odors and gas from the storage drain

5. Stainless steel safety clamp

6. Supporting pipe for stability

HEATHER KINKADE-LEVARIO

ABOVE LEFT:
Multisiphon overflow unit with floating ball to eliminate backflow of fluids and smells and the stainless steel grill prevents rodents from entering the tank
ABOVE RIGHT:
Residential pressure tanks supply pumped rainwater from the cistern to clothes washing machine and toilets

for this application, although the National Sanitation Foundation has not approved them for this purpose. If a 1-micron absolute filter is used, then a carbon filter should be installed to improve taste and odor. Most filters have been designed to be used with municipal supplies and do not have a convenient method of monitoring when they have become overloaded and are due for replacement. Filters connected to a cistern system should be changed more frequently than suggested by the manufacturer.

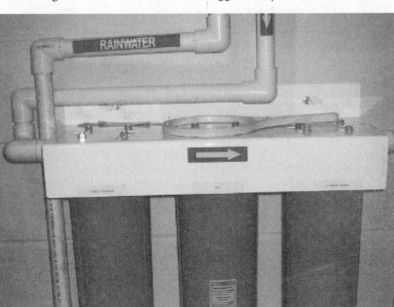

SHAWN HATLEY, BLUE RIDGE ATLANTIC ENTERPRISES

Rainwater filtration system

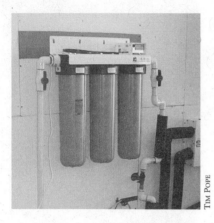

Left to right are 3 filters: a 5-micron sediment filter, a 0.5 micron carbon filter, and UV purification

TIM POPE

Solar water distillation systems are extremely energy efficient and are one of the simplest water purification systems available. The solar systems purify water using only the sun's energy. No filters or membranes are required, no moving parts are used, and no electricity is needed to run the solar distillation system. Solar water distillation systems consist of a shallow pan with a sloping glass cover. Rainwater to be purified by a solar system is directed to the pan where it is heated by the sun. The rainwater evaporates from the pan, rises, condenses on the underside of the glass cover, and runs down into a collection trough. From the trough the purified rainwater flows to a clean container for storage. The undesirable contaminants left behind in the pan are flushed from the pan daily. Solar distillation panels can be mounted on roofs or on ground structures.[22]

Rainwater quality is generally acceptable for potable use except when contaminated by organics such as leaves. Chemicals may be used to sterilize and purify the stored water. Rainwater used for potable systems should be periodically tested for quality and content. The quality of rainwater gathered for nonpotable uses, typically judged on the size of suspended solids, can be much lower. Nonpotable water needs to be devoid of suspended solids that may be too large to pass through the distribution system. With a drip irrigation system, additional filters can be used to avoid clogging the emitters.

Regular maintenance of all rainwater harvesting system components is required to provide optimal collection of rainwater. First-flush devices should be emptied after each storm, gutters should be clean and free of debris, and overflow lines should be free of obstacles that may block the pipe. Filters, pumps, and the cistern or storage container must be checked periodically to identify any loss of efficiency and to flush any debris that may have collected at the bottom. All piping and connections should be periodically inspected and repaired, if needed. All landscape channels, berms, and basins should be cleaned of nonorganic debris. Signs of erosion should be evaluated so that runoff can be stopped or redirected in order to increase percolation time. In addition, landscape irrigation emitters and plant basins should be expanded as plants and their roots grow.

System Complexity

The concept of rainwater harvesting has been explained, but before an actual system can be designed, several basic questions

CADO DAILY

HEATHER KINKADE-LEVARIO

must be answered and decisions reached regarding the system's size, complexity, cost, and intensity of use and purpose. Rainwater harvesting systems can be designed for small or large projects. They can retrofit an existing site or be an integral component of a new project. Designing a rainwater harvesting system for a new project has advantages, in both ease and cost, over retrofitting an existing building or site. A rainwater harvesting system can be designed as a passive, low-cost system or as an active, more complex and costly system. A decision needs to be made as to the intensity of use of a system and the intended use of the water, i.e., for nonpotable and/or for potable water.

The intended water demands must be evaluated through a water budget. During a rainy season the demand for water may be low, but during a dry season,

a high demand may be placed on the rainwater harvesting system. The quantity of water required during the dry periods or high demand times will determine the quantity of rainwater collected during rainy periods, which in turn will determine the cistern's storage capacity.

Storage capacity is one way to classify a rainwater harvesting system. A small system would have a storage capacity of 1,000 to 5,000 gallons, a medium system 5,001 to 10,000 gallons, a large system 10,001 to 25,000 gallons, with a very large system ranging up to 100,000 or 200,000 gallons and more. When determining the capacity needed, one should keep in mind the following atypical situations. In an area where uniform rainfall continually replenishes supplies, a rainwater harvesting system may have a small storage capacity and still be able to support high daily demand. However, in an area with long periods

Passive rainwater harvesting: landscape basin with low walls to slow runoff

Passive rainwater harvesting: butterfly roof drains to a cistern next to a garden

between rainfall, a rainwater harvesting system may need a very large storage capacity despite a low daily demand for water. The time period between rainfall events and number of times a user must rely on a rainwater harvesting system is known as the *intensity of use* of that system. Rainwater harvest-

ing systems can be additionally classified for intensity of use by the amount of water security or reliability provided by the system. Four levels of commitment to rainwater harvesting have been identified: [23, 24]

1. Occasional: this is typically a small storage capacity system

Lowe's Home Improvement Center that has four 18,100 gallon tanks

Fort Worth Botanical Gardens which has a 5,000-gallon TimberTank for irrigation of plants

that collects rainwater for one or two days of use. During a rainy period users will have the benefit of having most of their water needs, possibly all of their needs, met by the stored rainwater. An alternative water source would be required for dry weather. This system is best for climates with a uniform rainfall pattern and very few dry days between rainfall events.

2. Intermittent: this is typically a small- to medium-storage capacity system where the user's needs are met for a portion of the year. Dry periods may require an

alternate water source. This system is best for climates with a single rainy season, where it can meet most or all of a user's needs during that part of the year.

3. Partial: this is typically a medium- to large-storage capacity system. It provides some of the water needed for a landscape or all of the high-quality water needs, such as drinking water, for the user during the entire year. An alternative water source is needed to provide water for the remaining portion of the water needs for at least the historic dry season. This system is best in areas where a dependable, uniform rainfall occurs in a single or two short wet seasons.

4. Full: This is typically a large storage capacity system that provides all of the water needed by the user for the whole year. This may be the best option for areas with no alternate water source. It requires strict monitoring and regulated use of the water supply.

All factors classifying a rainwater harvesting system, including water supply demand, storage capacity, and intensity of use, can be determined and evaluated with the creation of a water budget, or water balance analysis.

Water Budget

A water balance analysis, typically referred to as a water budget, describes the amount of rainwater that can be collected in the project catchment area and determines if that amount will meet the user's water demands. A water budget will provide a supply-and-demand analysis on a monthly basis and will help determine the size of the storage area. In addition, a water budget will determine how much, if any, supplemental water is needed to augment the intended use of the collected rainwater.

The same budget steps can be completed for any specified water demand whether it is potable or nonpotable. If the water requirements are determined to be larger than the rainwater system

Passive rainwater harvesting: stepped walls to slow down runoff

HEATHER KINKADE-LEVARIO

is able to provide, and supplemental water is not wanted or cannot be used, the water budget will help determine how much the demand must be reduced to match the rainwater supplied. Redesigning a project to increase the catchment area, if possible, may be an option to increase the quantity of rainwater captured. An optional supplemental water supply, such as a well or municipal water, can serve as a security system for years of low rainfall or if a system needs servicing and the cistern requires draining. Because a water budget is based on average annual rainfall it will not be exact or guaranteed, but it should be used as a planning tool to help refine project goals as well as refine the water collection system and the intended water use.

A catchment area quantities table can be prepared on a gallons-per-month basis by using the average monthly rainfall for the site. When the catchment area is restricted and cannot be expanded, a conventional collection formula may be used to determine runoff quantities. The first step is to multiply the catchment area in square feet by the amount of rainfall received (expressed in feet). This quantity is then multiplied by the percent efficiency afforded by the collection surface and finally multiplied by 7.48, which is the number of gallons in a cubic foot. The result is the amount of rainwater collected from the catchment area. This first formula needs to be completed for each collection area and efficiency type, for each month. Catchment collection efficiencies have been estimated by various sources. Table 2.1 shows typical runoff efficiencies that have been proven appropriate for the construction material listed.

When the individual collection area boundaries are undefined, or if the collection areas are adjustable and/or the water available is on a budget, Formula 1 must be reconfigured (see Formula 2) to determine the area required for collection. When the required/allowed gallons of water per day are known, the first step is to multiply the gallons required per day by 365 days a year for the total water required per year for the project. The second step is to multiply the annual rainfall in inches by 0.623, which converts inches of rain into gallons per square foot of area (7.48 gallons per cubic foot divided by 12 inches equals 0.623). The third step is to divide the total gallons required per year by the gallons of rainwater collected per square foot per year. The resulting number is the catchment area in square feet required to collect, with 100 percent efficiency, the quantity of water required by the water budget.

After the catchment area is determined, the conventional formula can be completed to determine runoff supply for use in the water budget. A larger catchment area may be required to meet the water demand, depending on the runoff efficiencies of the catchment surface.

Table 2.2 shows an example of an available runoff supply for a typical 10-acre commercial project in Phoenix, Arizona using both rooftop and ground level catchment areas. Formula 1 was used to complete this table, using catchment areas of 94,520 square feet of roof area and 257,967 square feet of pavement area. The table can be expanded as appropriate for the number of catchment areas proposed. Once the potential water runoff supply is calculated, a table showing the water demand on a monthly basis and water supply (runoff) on a monthly basis can be prepared.

Formula 1. **Catchment area runoff in gallons**
(CA) x (R) x (E) x (7.48) = Catchment area runoff in gallons

Where:
CA = Catchment area (square feet)
R = Rainfall (expressed in feet)
E = Efficiency (See table 1)

Formula 2. **Total catchment area required in square feet**
[(TWR) x (365)] divided by [(AR) x (0.623)] = Total catchment area required in square feet

Where:
TWR = Total water required/allowed per day (gallons)
AR = Annual rainfall (inches)

Water Balance Analysis

This table, known as a water budget (Table 2.3), determines if the amount of rainwater collected meets the quantity required by the demand proposed or if supplemental make-up water from another source will be needed. A designer can use the maximum gallons harvested and recorded under the heading of accumulative storage, shown in the water budget, to calculate the volume and number of cisterns that will be required for the proposed project.

The largest quantity shown in the water budget for the available runoff supply will be the maximum gallons flowing through the storage system; however, a portion of the rainwater that has entered into storage will exit after the rain event, as irrigation in the Table 2.3 example. Therefore, the maximum accumulative gallons (or maximum stored gallons) shown in the water budget will be the amount used to size the storage system.

Consider pipe spacing inside a cistern or tank from the top of the cistern when preparing storage capacity calculations or

Table 2.1

ESTIMATED RUNOFF EFFICIENCIES

90%	Smooth, impervious roof surfaces, i.e., metal, tile, built-up and asphalt shingle roof.
80%	Gravel roof and paved surfaces.
60%	Treated soil.
30%	Natural soil.

Estimated runoff efficiencies for urban surfaces

when designing the inlet for a supplemental water supply. A cistern capacity should be calculated from the floor of the cistern to the invert of the overflow pipe. An overflow outlet pipe invert is typically provided 10 to 12 inches below the top of a cistern or tank, which means the top 10 to 12 inches is airspace and should not be calculated as storage capacity. Additional height will be required within the cistern for the inlet from downspouts and if an alternate make-up water source is proposed (Details 2.1 and 2.2). Some cisterns are based on gallons of capacity and others are based on cubic feet of storage. To determine the cubic foot capacity of a required cistern, Formula 3 can be used to change gallons to cubic feet of storage required. Formulas 4 and 5 can be used for sizing square and round cisterns and providing cubic feet of storage estimates.

A typical monthly landscape irrigation requirement for a typical 10-acre commercial project in Phoenix, Arizona was used to complete the water budget shown in Table 2.3. As the table demonstrates, if all the rooftop and pavement areas were used to harvest rainwater, an excess of rainwater would be collected. Thus, the water budget would not balance. Removing rooftop or pavement areas from the catchment quantities will reduce

Table 2.2

POTENTIAL RUNOFF SUPPLY

Month	Phoenix rainfall in feet	Rooftop collection at 90% efficiency in gallons	Pavement collection at 80% efficiency in gallons	Total
January	0.063	40,087	97,252	137,339
February	0.061	38,815	94,164	132,979
March	0.061	38,815	94,164	132,979
April	0.028	17,817	43,223	61,040
May	0.011	6,999	16,980	23,979
June	0.008	5,091	12,349	17,440
July	0.078	49,632	120,407	170,039
August	0.085	54,086	131,212	185,298
September	0.066	41,996	101,883	143,879
October	0.043	27,361	66,378	93,739
November	0.053	33,724	81,815	115,539
December	0.074	47,087	114,232	161,319
Annual	0.631	401,510	974,059	1,375,569

Potential runoff supply for each catchment area

the maximum accumulative storage of 443,431 gallons. Alternatively, the landscape areas could be increased to accommodate the use of more rainwater. To ensure a balanced budget for the typical project, a decision would need to be made to either increase the landscape areas or reduce the catchment size.

The water budget shown is for an established landscape. Newly planted vegetation will require supplemental water in addition to the harvested rainwater/stormwater during the plant establishment period. The plant

Table 2.3

TOTAL LANDSCAPE

	Irrigation requirement for established plants	Available runoff supply	Runoff minus landscape irrigation requirement	Excess runoff to storage requirement	Accumulative storage	Irrigation requirement from storage	Irrigation from municipal supply
January	41,748	137,339	95,591	95,591	329,377		0
February	58,076	132,979	74,903	74,903	404,280		0
March	93,828	132,979	39,151	39,151	443,431		0
April	131,867	61,040	-70,827	372,604	70,827		0
May	162,460	23,979	-138,481	234,123	138,481		0
June	179,897	17,440	-162,457	71,666	162,457		0
July	172,746	170,039	-2,707	68,959	2,707		0
August	153,744	185,298	31,554	31,544	31,554		0
September	126,407	143,879	17,472	17,472	49,026		0
October	93,828	93,739	-89	48,937	89		0
November	54,595	115,539	60,944	60,944	109,881		0
December	37,414	161,319	123,905	123,905	233,786		0
Total Annual Gallons	1,306,610	1,375,569	68,959	443,520	443,431	374,561	0

Water budget

Calculations were completed for the selected 10-acre commercial project in Phoenix.

Note: The above rainwater harvesting process was started in August with the summer rains in order to accumulate enough rainwater to fulfill the next summer's irrigation needs. The August quantity of 31,554 gallons begins the water budget/accumulative storage process. Each month as rainwater is harvested the quantity increases; during months that require water for irrigation above what is harvested for that month, the deficit is subtracted from the accumulative storage quantity. The accumulative storage is a running total of water in the cistern. The maximum amount of rainwater stored, 443,431 gallons, occurs in March. A cistern or storage facility is sized to hold the maximum accumulative quantity of rainwater plus a little extra as a safety factor or buffer for a non-average rainfall year.

establishment period would typically be two to five years, after which supplemental water would not be needed. The excess rainwater listed in the water budget could be used during the plant establishment period; once the plants are established, the catchment areas could be reduced to provide a balanced water budget.

The excess rainwater could also be allowed to recharge the aquifer by infiltrating through overflow outlet pipes to a landscape basin or a drywell.

Storage of the collected rainwater could be in above-ground or below-grade cisterns. The below-grade storage would be appropriate due to the valuable land needed to provide buildings and parking spaces and due to the large size of the maximum accumulated storage quantity.

The water budget for the selected typical 10-acre commercial project demonstrates how valuable a water budget can be in the planning phase of a project. It allows several options to be evaluated prior to selecting an appropriate ratio of catchment size or runoff quantity to water requirement.

Water Budget

Formula 3. **Determining cubic feet of water**
(Accumulative storage in gallons) divided by (7.48 gallons per cubic foot) = Cubic feet of storage required

Example:
(5,000 gallons accumulative storage) divided by (7.48 gallons per cubic foot) = 668 cubic feet of storage

Formula 4. **Sizing square or rectangular cisterns**
(Length) x (Width) x (Max. height of stored water) = Cubic feet of storage provided

Example:
10 feet long times 9 feet wide times 10 feet high = 900 cubic feet of storage provided

Formula 5. **Sizing round cisterns**
(πr^2) x (Max. height of stored water) = Cubic feet of storage

Where:
π = 3.14
r^2 = Radius of cistern squared

Example:
3.14 times 5-foot radius squared times 10-foot height = 785 cubic feet available for storage

Cold Weather Considerations

Winter hydrologic conditions—ice, freezing temperatures, snow, and snowmelt—present special considerations for water collection and stormwater runoff. With freshly fallen snow, 10 inches of snow equals approximately 0.7 inches of water; another way to calculate it is that 14 inches of snow equals 1 inch of water. Over time, the snow becomes more compacted and by the time it begins to melt it will yield more water per inch. In this case, 3 to 4 inches of snow will equal 1 inch of water.

The list below addresses a few of the considerations required for cold climates.

Tanks: Larger tanks are recommended as a large tank will take longer to freeze than a small one; a round tank is recommended as a round tank will lose heat more slowly than a rectangular one of the same volume; straight sides are recommended as corrugated sides have more surface area; insulation is recommended, e.g., spray-on polyurethane foam; tank roofs should be designed to withstand heavier loads such as snow and a steep-angle roof allows the snow to slide off faster; a central tank roof support is recommended for additional strength; tanks should be designed to take into account the rising and falling water surface level and internal fittings—ladders attached to walls—should be avoided.[25]

Tank Water: In cold water settling velocities are up to 50 percent slower; [26] higher pollutant levels maybe experienced in the water as the pollutants—such as ash from fireplace use—will likely build up during the cold season and when melt does occur, larger quantities of runoff water may be experienced; [27] during deep-freeze conditions moving water is less likely to freeze than standing water and the water in the tank may need to be constantly cycled to prevent freezing, possibly cycled through a solar hot water system.[28]

Pipes: If possible pipes should be buried below the freeze line; pipe distribution points should be located as close to the use as possible and preferably inside a building; using suitable piping materials will reduce the probability of pipes splitting; Medium Density Polyethylene (MDPE) remains ductile even at lower temperatures (health implications of drinking water filtration requirements is unknown and water quality should be evaluated with all piping materials), and the typical warm-weather PVC pipe is more brittle at lower temperatures; if the system is not used during cold periods, the pipes should be drained.[29]

Wooden tank construction in cold climate — base

Wooden tank construction in cold climate — sides

Wooden tank construction in cold climate — roof

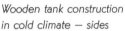

Valves: Valves can be protected by being placed in insulated boxes.[30]

Tank Foundations: Heat loss from the water in the tank to the ground may occur causing the soil below the water to thaw quicker causing structural instability; mounting a tank on an insulated concrete or gravel base will reduce the heat transfer.[31]

Pumps: The fact that engine fluids thicken at lower temperatures should be taken into account and appropriate diesels and oils should be used; pumps should be protected in a pump house or insulated box.[32]

Chlorination: The reaction

Tank in the high mountains

Tank located at 9,000 feet elevation near Aspen, Colorado, in the snow

rate of chlorination is seriously affected at lower temperatures, if this is a technique used for purification, more time may be required for the purification/reaction time.[33]

Cold climates cause more concern for maintenance as the tank, pipes, valves, and other components of a system such as the roof of an above-grade tank need to be inspected more often to evaluate conditions and potential stress points. This list is a beginning and some items may have been overlooked as every site is unique and may have special issues to be evaluated.

The Alaskan Building Research Series HCM-01557,

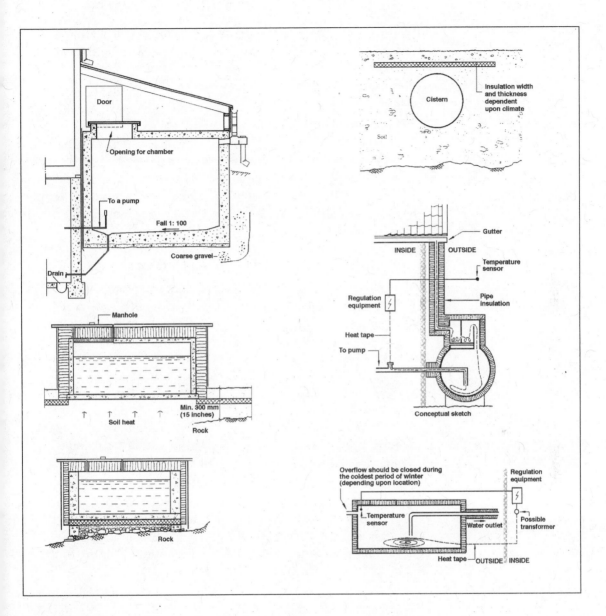

Labels within figure:

Door

Opening for chamber

To a pump

Fall 1: 100

Coarse gravel

Drain

Manhole

Min. 300 mm (15 inches)

Soil heat

Rock

Rock

Cistern

Insulation width and thickness dependent upon climate

Soil

Gutter

INSIDE   OUTSIDE

Temperature sensor

Pipe insulation

Regulation equipment

Heat tape

To pump

Conceptual sketch

Overflow should be closed during the coldest period of winter (depending upon location)

Temperature sensor

Regulation equipment

Possible transformer

Water outlet

Heat tape   OUTSIDE   INSIDE

Cold weather details

Left: top to bottom:
- Cistern built partially above ground.
- Frost protection using the soil geothermal heat (in nonpermafrost areas only).
- Frost protection of cistern on rock.

Right: top to bottom:
- If excavation to frost free depth is extreme, the ground above the cistern can be insulated with blueboard or similar.
- Frost protection can consist of pipe insulation and heat tape within pipes and the cistern.
- Frost protection of cistern with heat tape, note temperature sensor is placed inside the cistern.

(Source: *Water Cistern Construction for Small Houses*, Alaska Building Research Series HCM-01557)

Water Cistern Construction for Small Houses, lists a few good points to be addressed when using cisterns in cold climates. Those points are as follows:

- In nonpermafrost areas an above-grade cistern may only need side and top insulation, as soil heat may be enough to keep the water from freezing.

- If a cistern is placed on solid rock, soil warming of the cistern water is unlikely and the cistern bottom should be insulated.

- Insulation of square or rectangular cisterns should use boards of extruded polystyrene due to their moisture-resistant properties. Cylindrical cisterns should be insulated with batt insulation and a Visqueen (polyethylene) outer layer.

- If a cistern is located below-grade it needs to be placed below the freeze depth to avoid frost/freeze problems. If this is an extreme depth, an option would be to insulate the ground above the cistern.

The necessary depth of soil cover will relate to the thickness of the insulation.

- All pipes should be insulated and heat tape threaded inside the pipes or wrapped around them. Heat tapes can be placed in loops on the bottom of the cistern as well as around the intake. An automatic thermostat with a temperature sensor placed inside the cistern should be used to turn the heat tapes on and off.

- Heat tapes can be used on downspouts, gutters, and along the roof eaves to avoid frozen systems and allow water collection to be continued during cold times. The storage system can also be disconnected from the collection components during the winter if no collection is needed or desired.

- Summer cisterns should always be emptied, cleaned, and decommissioned (including disconnecting downspouts) for the winter season.

3 Passive Rainwater and Stormwater Catchment

THIS CHAPTER describes passive rainwater and stormwater catchment techniques and components. Passive rainwater collection, using such techniques as site grading and permeable surfaces, diverts and retains stormwater so that it benefits the landscaped elements of a site. Details provided in this chapter are meant to be starting points for a passive system; individual systems and components should be customized for specific sites. Active rainwater collection, described in previous chapters, not only diverts the stormwater, but also stores it for later use. It makes use of such features as architectural amenities, first-flush diverters, and storage systems. Details for active systems are provided in Chapter Four.

A More Natural Approach

Using proper techniques, both on-site runoff and off-site flows can be caught using passive means. Planning for this type of water catchment requires an integrated design process where all team members—including the owner, planner, developer, engineer, architect, landscape architect, contractor, and maintenance personnel—work together to attain an effective collection system. The following pages describe and illustrate various techniques that can be used.

Passive water collection starts by managing stormwater at the top of the watershed. A project might have multiple micro watersheds within its boundaries, all of which can assist in slowing

Landscape swale after a spring rain

HEATHER KINKADE-LEVARIO

Passive rainwater harvesting: landscape retention basin

Passive rainwater harvesting: curb cut allows rainwater from street gutter to enter landscaped/natural desert area

Passive rainwater harvesting: curb cut allows surface flow to enter landscape basin

percolate more when its velocity is reduced and it is spread out over a permeable surface.

There are numerous ways to slow and direct stormwater, including microbasins, swales, French drains, rain gardens, permeable pavements, and curb and road grading design. To prevent the possible destabilization of sloped areas, it is best to consult an engineer if any of these techniques are used on or adjacent to slopes over 10 percent.

A more natural approach to land development is needed to mimic natural cycles, especially the hydrological cycle. In an undisturbed environment almost all rain and snowmelt soak into the ground where it falls and only the heavier rains exceed infiltration rates to produce surface runoff. The gentle sustained infiltration supports plant life, maximizes groundwater recharge, and minimizes flooding and erosion.

Collecting and storing water in the soil, above the water table, is a process that increases "green" water levels. Increasing soil moisture means less water needs to be artificially applied to a landscape to maintain its existence. In an urban setting much of the land surface is covered with impervious surfaces, surfaces that disconnect the natural hydrologic cycle. These impermeable surfaces increase runoff velocities, therefore increasing erosion and flooding hazards.

and spreading the stormwater. Proper site grading can make maximum use of watersheds. Stormwater will erode less soil and

There are several existing examples of this more natural approach, including a technique also known as Low Impact Development, or LID. The most well known example is the 1999 manual prepared by Prince Georges County, Maryland, Department of Environmental Resources entitled *Low Impact Development Design Strategies: An Integrated Design Approach.* More can be found on this topic at the Low Impact Development Center website www.lowimpact development.org.

The City of Portland is one municipality that has made a commitment to provide a more natural approach to stormwater management. An example of their commitment is demonstrated in their Green Streets program. This program converts

Heather Kinkade-Levario

previously underutilized landscape areas adjacent to streets into a series of landscaped stormwater planters that are designed to accept street runoff, slow it, cleanse it, and infiltrate it. Excessive runoff exits one planter, only to enter the next. Eventually, if the quantity of stormwater entering the basins exceeds the soil's holding capacity, the

Passive rainwater harvesting: permeable pavement (pavers) used to identify parking spaces

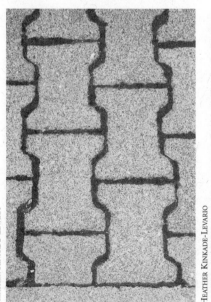

Heather Kinkade-Levario

Heather Kinkade-Levario

LEFT:
Passive rainwater harvesting: permeable pavement (pavers)
RIGHT:
Passive rainwater harvesting: drain at base of steps leads to adjacent landscaped area

Passive rainwater harvesting: landscape basin for runoff infiltration

stormwater is allowed to enter storm drains, but at a much delayed rate and in a much cleaner state.

This retrofit of street curbs and landscape planters manage what were typically direct flows of street runoff to storm drains that originally fed directly into the Willamette River. The City of Portland Environmental Services has prepared a manual

dated November 2003 titled: *Sustainable Site Development, Stormwater Practices For New, Redevelopment, and Infill Projects.* This manual lists eight actions, benefits of each action, and justification for each action. Listed below are the eight actions:

1. Manage stormwater as close to the source as possible to reduce or eliminate the volume of water and pollutants leaving the site. Integrate stormwater into site development, building, and landscape design.

2. Preserve, protect, and plant trees and vegetation. Increase use of native trees and vegetation.

3. Reduce impacts from impervious surfaces such as streets, parking lots, rooftops, and

Green Streets Project: signage

LEFT:
Green Streets Project:
view looking uphill
RIGHT:
Green Streets Project:
view looking downhill

Green Streets Project: inlet
with asphalt diversion dam

other paved surfaces.

4. Avoid disruption along stream corridors. Create vegetative buffers.

5. Avoid development in the floodplain and restore natural floodplain functions.

6. Prevent and control erosion caused by construction and routine site development activities such as clearing and grading.

7. Locate and design streets to protect stream corridors and reduce high flows and polluted runoff.

8. Educate and enlist local agencies and the community

Green Streets Project: end with stormdrain

Passive rainwater harvesting: permeable parking lot

in these guiding principles and actions.

Details for Passive Collection

There are numerous ways to capture and maintain stormwater on a site. Rooftop water can be captured and stored for future irrigation use or for non-landscape uses, which will eliminate the captured water quantity from runoff calculations allowing only surface runoff to be dealt with through passive approaches.

Microbasins are small catchment areas that are best for low volumes of stormwater. By slowing stormwater, they allow infiltration rates to increase.

Heather Kinkade-Levario

Heather Kinkade-Levario

Passive rainwater harvesting: permeable parking lot driveway

University of Arizona, Tucson, Arizona stepped stormwater basins adjacent to a building, note gutter down-spouts feed each basin

They can be located in a line or in an alternating pattern that allows overflow to be repeatedly slowed to allow additional infiltration. The microbasins can be tree wells, planter islands—with curb cuts allowing stormwater to enter similar to the Green Streets Program—or just small depressions next to a path or drive.

Swales are gently sloping trenches meant to slow sheet flow and to allow longer standing/infiltration periods. They are best for low to medium volumes of stormwater. Swales can be located next to sidewalks, paths, and driveways—typically they direct stormwater towards vegetation and away from buildings.

Heather Kinkade-Levario

Passive rainwater harvesting: sidewalk drain

Additional passive rainwater harvesting: sidewalk drain

Heather Kinkade-Levario

They can vary greatly in width and treatment, from small short depressions to long trenches graded across a site requiring the use of heavy equipment. Swales are typically graded with the contours or perpendicular to the flowing water.

French drains and rain gardens are designed to absorb stormwater rapidly from the surface. French drains and pumice wicks are rock-filled excavations that lead to below-grade storage or infiltration areas. They can be dug vertically or horizontally in the earth, and they may be referred to as soak-a-ways or drywells. Rain gardens are landscaped areas that are designed to direct stormwater to a central storage or infiltration area.

Permeable pavement can also be used to slow stormwater and allow more infiltration to

occur. Streets, patios, sidewalks, crosswalks, and parking lots can consist of pavers that allow stormwater to pass between them to sand or gravel sub-base layers that lead to a natural soil sub-base material.

Finally, passive rainwater and stormwater collection techniques can include the grading of a site to allow stormwater to pass over or through curbs to enter depressed, and typically landscaped, planter islands in parking lots or adjacent landscaped tracts. Sidewalks and driveways can be graded towards a landscaped area instead of towards a storm drain. These landscaped islands and tracts can be designed as individual rain gardens or just as a typical landscape area. Either way the additional stormwater runoff will benefit the existing vegetation.

*Passive rainwater harvesting:
green roof on a library
in Salt Lake, UT*

*Passive rainwater harvesting:
green roof on church
in Salt Lake, UT*

*Passive rainwater harvesting:
drainage swale next
to sidewalk*

Passive rainwater harvesting: curb cut to allow stormwater runoff into infiltration cell

Passive rainwater harvesting: infiltration cells next to trees

Microbasins

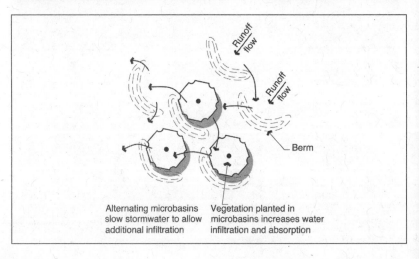

Runoff flow

Runoff flow

Berm

Alternating microbasins slow stormwater to allow additional infiltration

Vegetation planted in microbasins increases water infiltration and absorption

Stepped stormwater basins manage overflow from other basins fed from downspout drains

Swales

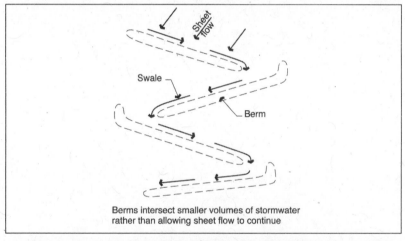

Sheet flow

Swale

Berm

Berms intersect smaller volumes of stormwater rather than allowing sheet flow to continue

Passive rainwater harvesting: rock weir on a swale

Infiltration swale fed by adjacent parking lot drain, hidden from adjacent street by berm and vegetation

French drains

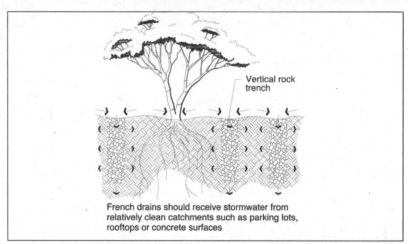

Vertical rock trench

French drains should receive stormwater from relatively clean catchments such as parking lots, rooftops or concrete surfaces

Passive rainwater harvesting: gutters extend from the building to drop rainwater into a permeable channel for infiltration and irrigation of adjacent vegetation

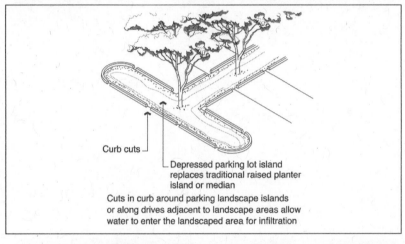

Curb cuts

Depressed parking lot island
replaces traditional raised planter
island or median

Cuts in curb around parking landscape islands
or along drives adjacent to landscape areas allow
water to enter the landscaped area for infiltration

*Passive rainwater harvesting:
permeable channel below
the extended gutters*

*Depressed parking lot
landscape island*

*Passive rainwater harvesting:
infiltration cells with weirs*

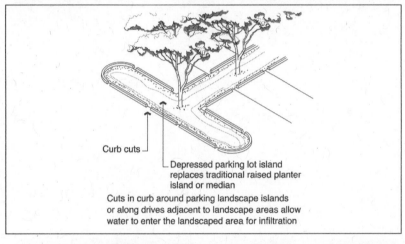

HEATHER KINKADE-LEVARIO

HEATHER KINKADE-LEVARIO

Passive rainwater harvesting: parking lot basin accepts site runoff and irrigates vegetation

Sidewalk grading

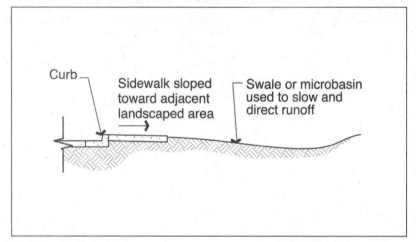

Curb

Sidewalk sloped toward adjacent landscaped area

Swale or microbasin used to slow and direct runoff

LEFT:
Passive rainwater harvesting: entry driveway curbs are flush with asphalt to allow runoff to enter landscape
RIGHT:
Passive rainwater harvesting: church parking lot median without curb allows runoff to enter basin; basin is then stepped to detain water until it has had an extended time to infiltrate the landscape

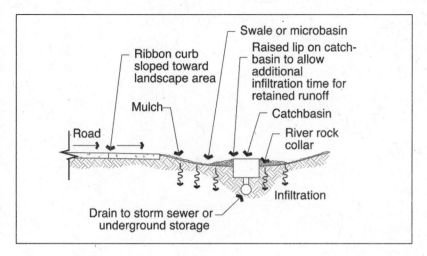

Ribbon curb sloped toward landscape area

Mulch

Road

Drain to storm sewer or underground storage

Swale or microbasin

Raised lip on catch-basin to allow additional infiltration time for retained runoff

Catchbasin

River rock collar

Infiltration

Roadway grading

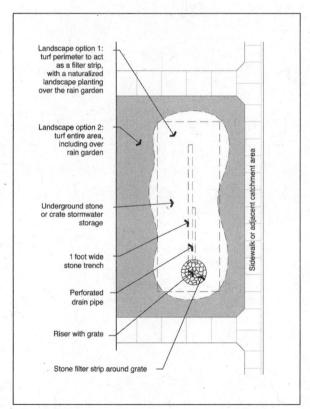

Landscape option 1: turf perimeter to act as a filter strip, with a naturalized landscape planting over the rain garden

Landscape option 2: turf entire area, including over rain garden

Underground stone or crate stormwater storage

1 foot wide stone trench

Perforated drain pipe

Riser with grate

Stone filter strip around grate

Sidewalk or adjacent catchment area

Rain garden, plan view

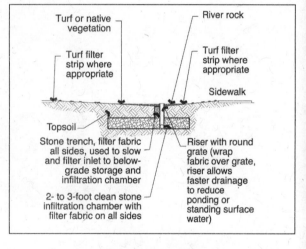

Turf or native vegetation

Turf filter strip where appropriate

Topsoil

Stone trench, filter fabric all sides, used to slow and filter inlet to below-grade storage and infiltration chamber

2- to 3-foot clean stone infiltration chamber with filter fabric on all sides

River rock

Turf filter strip where appropriate

Sidewalk

Riser with round grate (wrap fabric over grate, riser allows faster drainage to reduce ponding or standing surface water)

Rain garden, section view with natural stone

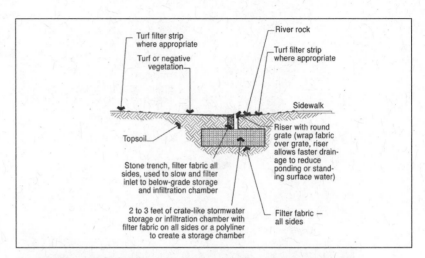

Turf filter strip where appropriate

Turf or negative vegetation

River rock

Turf filter strip where appropriate

Sidewalk

Topsoil

Riser with round grate (wrap fabric over grate, riser allows faster drainage to reduce ponding or standing surface water)

Stone trench, filter fabric all sides, used to slow and filter inlet to below-grade storage and infiltration chamber

2 to 3 feet of crate-like stormwater storage or infiltration chamber with filter fabric on all sides or a polyliner to create a storage chamber

Filter fabric — all sides

Rain garden, section view with crates

Passive rainwater harvesting: rain garden with curb cuts to allow round-about runoff water into the landscape for infiltration and passive irrigation

Concrete Unit Pavers

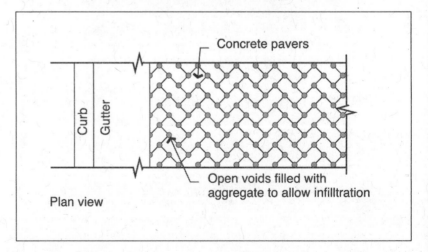

Concrete pavers

Curb

Gutter

Open voids filled with aggregate to allow infiltration

Plan view

MAINTENANCE OF PASSIVE RAINWATER AND STORMWATER FEATURES

1. Keep microbasins and swales free of debris while maintaining surface mulch. (Mulch reduces evaporation.)

2. Block and/or repair any erosion trails that develop at overflows and spillways.

3. As plants grow, expand basins feeding them to encourage wide root development.

4. Augment active rainwater system with an alternate water source until plants are established, then wean plants off irrigation water.

5. Fine-tune landscape contours to control spillways, aesthetics, and functionality.

6. Inspect site before and after each rain event.

7. Keep mud and sediment out of French drains and wick areas. If possible, use with only roof-top runoff or use vegetated swales or basins to remove sediment prior to water entering French drains.

8. Inspect rain gardens for failure or unwanted erosion prior to and after each rain event. Maintain clear riser grates and stone trenches.

9. Sweep permeable pavers with a street-sweeping machine every three to five years; follow manufacturer's guidelines.

Heather Kinkade-Levario

Passive rainwater harvesting: concrete unit pavers

LEFT:
Passive rainwater harvesting: curb cuts on commercial site allow runoff to enter landscaped area
RIGHT:
Passive rainwater harvesting: curb cuts at entry drive allow runoff to return to desert vegetation

Heather Kinkade-Levario

Heather Kinkade-Levario

4 Equipment for an Active Rainwater Catchment System

THIS CHAPTER provides information on all the components involved in an active water catchment system. Each component is initially discussed in general, then maintenance information is itemized, and details are provided for better understanding of the individual components.

Rooftops, Gutters, and Downspouts

Rooftops, gutters, and downspouts can capture and direct rainfall and protect buildings from water damage. Gutters and downspouts also transport rainwater away from sensitive areas such as doors, walkways, and protected soils. Gutters are typically only used on residential buildings, but downspouts are used on both residential and commercial buildings.

When buying metal gutters, choose the thickest metal available and look for primary or virgin materials. Secondary or

> *….Good luck and good work for the happy mountain raindrops, each one of them a high waterfall in itself, descending from the cliffs and hollows of the clouds to the cliffs and hollows of the rocks, out of the sky – thunder into the thunder of the falling rivers.*
>
> — John Muir

Butterfly roof on garage

HEATHER KINKADE-LEVARIO

Sandy Murdoch, Rain Harvesting Pty Ltd

Heather Kinkade-Levario

LEFT:
Blue Mountain Mesh all
steel gutter mesh
on corrugated roof
RIGHT:
Red clay tile roof

recycled materials are often inconsistent in thickness and may contain dissolvable non-potable substances. Thin materials may be damaged or crushed by falling branches or ladders that are leaned up against them, though damage through maintenance can be avoided by careful use of ladders and other maintenance equipment. Vinyl or plastic gutters are susceptible to damage by maintenance equipment, but are impervious to rust and rot. Vinyl gutters can also become brittle in extreme hot and cold climates. Steel and aluminum gutters are the most common materials used in residential systems. Galvanized steel gutters are the most economical choice and are stronger than aluminum gutters, but they may eventually rust. Stainless steel gutters, though they are the most expensive, are the strongest, remain rust-free, and maintain a high sheen for years.

All gutter sections should be attached to downspouts via drop outlets, and should have end caps and corner pieces. Individual gutter sections can be connected or joined with snap-in-place connectors. Joining two sections of gutter together always allows a potential spot for leaks: the use of seamless or continuous gutter will help to eliminate this problem. Gutters come in numerous shapes, sizes, and colors. Downspouts are typically round or square and can match the gutter color.

Gutter covers and protectors defend the gutter from potential clogging and sagging due to debris weight or standing water caused by items that may enter the gutter, such as plant materials, animals, or toys. They can be found in numerous forms, including snap-on screens, grates, louvered (stepped or slotted filters), and helmet-like (which allow rainwater to enter

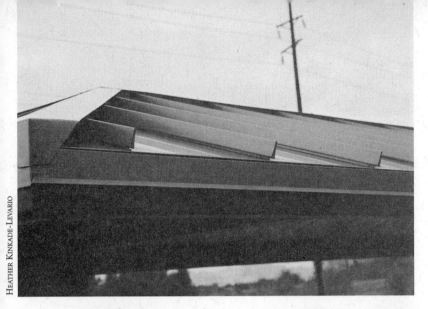

*Standing seam
metal roof*

*Grey flat
tile roof*

through a thin linear slot between gutter and cover).

There is a wide variety of suitable roofing material, but be aware that copper roofs are not suggested for any type of collection system. Galvanized roofs, which contain zinc, are likewise not appropriate for potable collection systems.

MAINTENANCE OF ROOF GUTTERS AND DOWNSPOUTS

1. Conduct a visual inspection of gutters and downspouts every six months to ensure that all clips and brackets are secure and not broken. Any broken or missing components should be repaired. Check slope of gutters to maintain positive drainage.

Gutter end

2. At six-month intervals remove accumulated debris and clogs. Where vegetation overhangs gutters, inspect them every three months for leaf accumulation, rust, and mold.

3. Inspect gutter system before and after each rainy season.

4. Trim trees and vines away from gutters to maintain a minimum 24-inch clear zone.

5. When gutter covers are used, inspect to eliminate any openings that may allow birds or other animals to enter and build nests. Inspect all cover clips to ensure the guards will not collapse and cause a blockage in the system. Inspect gutter cover for debris accumulation; dry accumulated debris may become a fire hazard and must be eliminated.

6. Downspouts and outlets located in landscape areas should be inspected every six months to ensure that splash pad placement is correct and that there is posi-tive drainage away from the outlet and adjacent buildings; maintain a minimum of 2 percent slope for the first 5 feet. Check for animal inhabitations and clogs. Check landscape growth every two weeks during growing periods to protect from overgrowth, which could obstruct positive drainage.

7. Flush gutters and downspouts once all debris is removed to wash away any remaining dirt or materials.

8. Keep subsurface drains clear of debris. Remove all accumulated mud or dirt that could enter drainage system.

Roofs can occasionally grow moss, and it should be dealt with immediately in a manner that will not degrade collected rainwater. Downspouts should be disconnected during the demossing process. More information on demossing can be found at www.uaf.edu/coop-ext/

Downspout attached to a gutter

Gutter

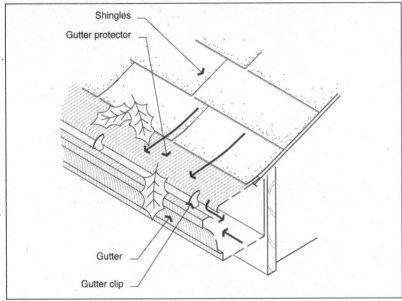

Shingles

Gutter protector

Gutter

Gutter clip

publications (search: demossing); at www.pesticide.org / roofmoss.pdf; and at www.cleanwaterservices.org.

Downspout Filters

Downspout filters such as the Leaf Beater® and the Leaf Eater® provide a second chance to capture and remove debris that might enter a rainwater storage system. They can be used inline prior to a roof washer or first-flush diverter. First-flush devices isolate the first runoff from a catchment surface while allowing the additional runoff to pass by. They can use floating balls, sinking balls, flaps, or can be based on the capacity of a vessel.

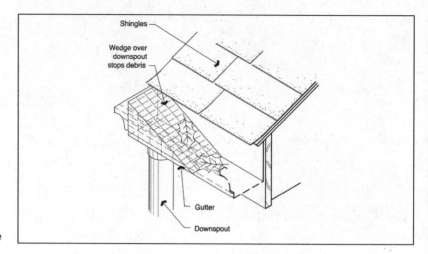

Gutter wedge

Snap-on gutter protector

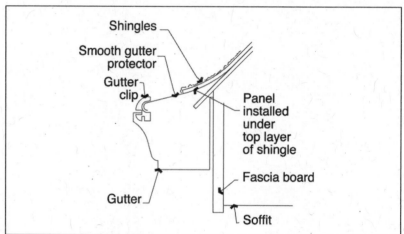

Perforated gutter protector with mesh screen

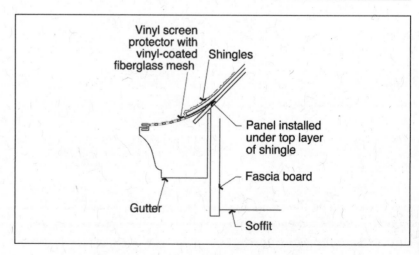

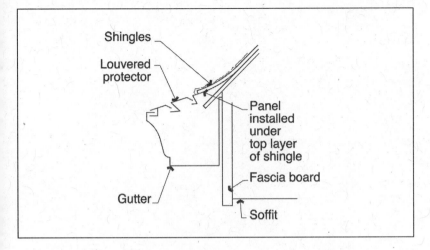

Shingles

Louvered protector

Panel installed under top layer of shingle

Fascia board

Gutter

Soffit

Louvered gutter protector

Helmet-like gutter protector

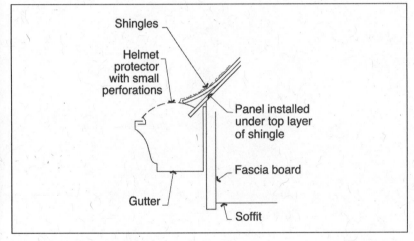

Shingles

Helmet protector with small perforations

Panel installed under top layer of shingle

Fascia board

Gutter

Soffit

A sand filter is an option for filtering rainwater prior to storage. Sand and gravel will remove some contaminants, and if combined with limestone, the acidic nature of the rainwater will be neutralized. A sand filter requires backwashing regularly to discourage bacterial growth that can create a crust layer on the sand and cause clogging of the sand's top layer. Sediment will add to the clogging. The sand should periodically be replaced with new sand. The sand used in these filters should be washed, screened beach or quarry sand. The filter should also have a large surface area with the outlet pipe equaling the inlet pipe size.

MAINTENANCE OF DOWNSPOUT FILTERS

1. Clean filter with warm soapy water or rinse well every three to six months.

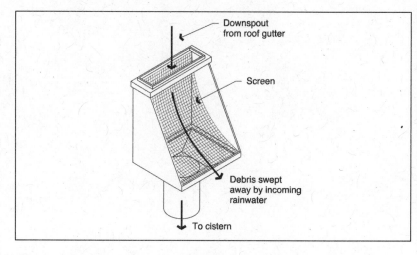

Australian Leaf Beater®
Rain Head
A high-performance rain
head with adjustable
elliptical primary screen.
Contains interior stain-
less steel low-flow-rate
secondary screen for
use when connected to
an under-eaves tank
SOURCE:
Adapted from Rain
Harvesting Pty Ltd. 2006

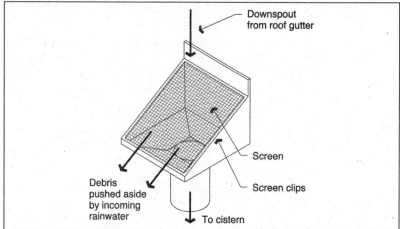

Australian Leaf Eater®
Rain Head
A high performance rain
head for heavy rainfall
areas—also used as a debris-
removing device in urban
areas. Contains primary and
secondary screens.
SOURCE:
Adapted from Rain
Harvesting Pty Ltd. 2006

2. Check that the drop from gutter remains vertical. Check to ensure that the bulk of water is landing centrally and towards the back of the leaf and debris filter screen.

3. Check for any obstructions and signs of damage to the leaf and debris filter.

First-flush Devices and Roof Washers

First-flush devices range in size to meet the demand of the rain-water catchment system. These diversion devices can be part of the downspout, be separate from a tank or cistern, or be attached to a tank or cistern. They can be below grade for large stormwater collection systems, where the harvested water is used for nonpotable purposes such as landscape irrigation, carwash supply, or toilet flushing. The size and volume depend on the amount of water being diverted

First-flush on a Hawaiian rainwater tank

LEFT:
Typical standpipe
RIGHT:
SafeRain© Vertical Diversion Valve

to a storage system and the ultimate use of the harvested water.

For any first-flush diversion device to work efficiently—especially for potable systems—the contaminated water must be sealed off so the rainwater flowing on to the storage cistern(s) does not siphon off the contaminated water from the first-flush device chamber.

First-flush diverters should operate on a predetermined and set volume and the contaminated water should be sealed off from the flow of clean water. First-flush diverters that operate on an estimated open flow rate are typically accurate enough to guarantee that most bacteria have been flushed from the roof

Guidelines for residential first-flush quantities

Rooftops of 1,000 square feet or smaller . . . . 5–10 gallons

Rooftops of 1,000 square feet or larger . . . . 10 gallons/1,000 square feet

Guidelines for surface catchment or for very large rooftops

Rooftop or surface catchment of 43,560 square feet or larger . . . . 500 gallons

(1,000 gallons if surface contains excessive soil, dust, or debris). Multiple first-flush devices instead of a larger first-flush may be required depending on slope of the catchment surface and time required for rainwater to reach the first-flush device.

prior to closure. Since the goal is to not waste valuable clean water, the most efficient and safest way to ensure that the appropriate amount of water is diverted is to assess the contamination on the

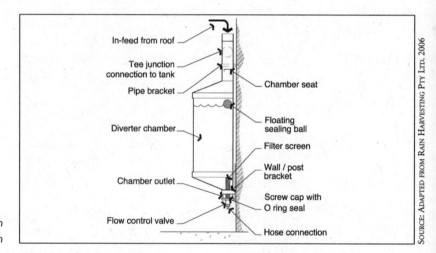

Australian first-flush

SOURCE: ADAPTED FROM RAIN HARVESTING PTY LTD. 2006

Baffle first-flush

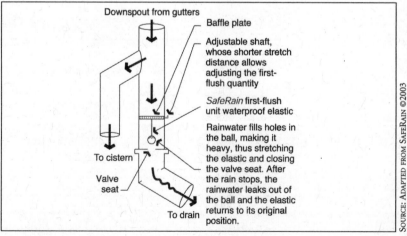

SOURCE: ADAPTED FROM SAFERAIN ©2003

roof and calculate a diversion amount based on that assessment. A set pre-sized diverter chamber with a free-floating ball and seat incorporating a flow control release valve is the optimum diversion unit.

If the water diverter does not have a self-sealing device, it is best to have it drop off a horizontal length of pipe away from the downspout so that the roof water does not drop directly into the water diverter and pick up contaminants as it travels to the cistern.

MAINTENANCE OF FIRST-FLUSH DEVICES AND ROOF WASHERS

1. Contaminated water in the first-flush device should be drained either manually or automatically after each rainfall event.

2. Check for clogs and working ability of roof washers prior to rainy season.

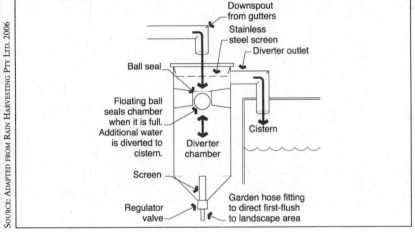

Floating ball first-flush

Typical stand-pipe first-flush

3. If device is not self-cleaning, check roof washers immediately after each rainfall event to empty any standing water.

4. Large below-grade systems should allow evaporation or filtration of first-flush water.

5. If petroleum-absorbent pillows are added to the first-flush chamber they should be evaluated for saturation/absorption capacity every year to determine quantity of materials washed off the catchment surface to the first-flush device. Multiple petroleum pillows may be needed; follow manufacturer's guidelines.

6. Large first-flush devices should be evaluated yearly for sediment and debris content, and cleaned if needed.

7. Debris shields and vegetation traps should be evaluated to guarantee unrestricted flows prior to rainy seasons.

First-flush location without a self-sealing device

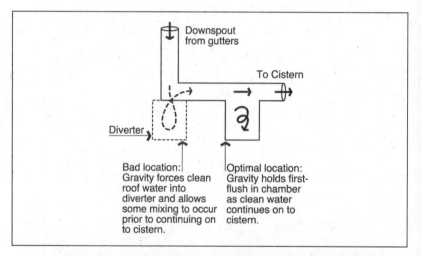

Downspout from gutters

To Cistern

Diverter

Bad location: Gravity forces clean roof water into diverter and allows some mixing to occur prior to continuing on to cistern.

Optimal location: Gravity holds first-flush in chamber as clean water continues on to cistern.

Equipment below-ground access

Debris basket lid

Debris basket

Downspout Diversion to a Rainbarrel or Rainchain

Rainbarrels collect rainwater for nonpotable uses. Even the lightest of rainfall can fill a rainbarrel. Rainbarrels should have a top mesh screen or a plastic lid to act as a barrier to mosquitos. Even with barriers, insect eggs may enter a barrel with rainwater that has been sitting on a catchment surface or in a gutter for a period of time.

Mosquito dunks can be used in rainbarrels as well as in a cistern to kill mosquito larva. It is recommended that gutter guards or protectors and leaf screens be used prior to rainbarrel storage. Rainbarrels should be equipped with overflow outlets, hose connections, multiple barrel attachment devices, and a drain plug, and should be placed on a stable foundation.

Rainchains should be securely attached to the gutter and, in potentially windy areas, attached to the ground.

MAINTENANCE OF RAINBARRELS AND RAINCHAINS

1. Check rainbarrel before rainy season to ensure overflow is clear and directed to the appropriate location.

2. Check rainbarrel before rainy season for leaks and cracks, and check all connection hoses for wear.

3. Check rainbarrel top mesh for holes and debris accumulation. Remove all obstructions and replace torn screens.

4. Add mosquito dunk as recommended by manufacturer for the capacity of rainbarrel.

5. Regularly inspect rainchain connections at gutter and ground level for wear and tear and to guarantee positive drainage.

6. If rainchains are leading rainwater to a subsurface drain,

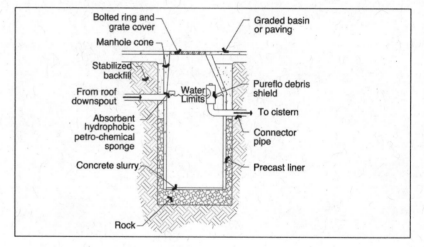

Below-grade drywell first-flush conversion (for nonpotable use)

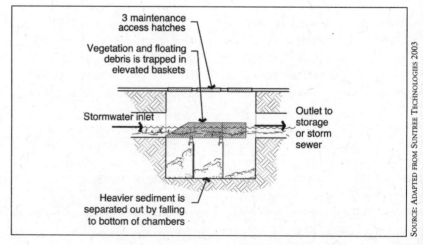

Below-grade stormwater first-flush (for nonpotable use)

SOURCE: ADAPTED FROM SUNTREE TECHNOLOGIES 2003

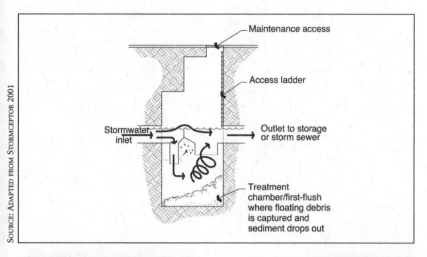

SOURCE: ADAPTED FROM STORMCEPTOR 2001

- Maintenance access
- Access ladder
Stormwater inlet
- Outlet to storage or storm sewer
- Treatment chamber/first-flush where floating debris is captured and sediment drops out

Below-grade storm-water first-flush (for nonpotable use)

LEFT:
Rainchain at spa
RIGHT:
Rainchain from extended gutter at spa

HEATHER KINKADE-LEVARIO

HEATHER KINKADE-LEVARIO

inspect drain inlet for debris accumulation.

7. Inspect splash pad for proper placement and positive drainage away from adjacent buildings.

Storage Systems

Cisterns and tanks on the market range widely in size and material. No matter what type of storage system is selected, the base or footing must be level and compacted. Steel tanks, which contain liners, typically require a concrete base. Concrete, fiberglass, or plastic tanks do not require a concrete base or a liner. Some sites will not accommodate large storage units below the elevation of the

LEFT:
Rainchain directing rainwater to below-ground storage
RIGHT:
Butterfly roof, rainchain, and splash pad on commercial building

structure or surface receiving the rainwater and therefore require a smaller storage unit from which the initially harvested water can be pumped to the main units.

Tanks and cisterns are not meant to be airtight. Some venting is required to allow pressure adjustments in the storage system. Below-grade tanks and cisterns must be able to withstand surface loads. One-piece units should be tested for leakage prior to installation.

Permanent-access ladders to above- or below-grade tanks and cisterns are optional.

Pumps may be required: if tanks are below-grade; if there is insufficient gravity to feed the demand; if the captured water needs to be distributed to a higher elevation; or if the water needs to be distributed under pressure. A qualified plumber should be consulted to set pump types and sizes. Typically in potable systems a floating pump intake,

Rain cups

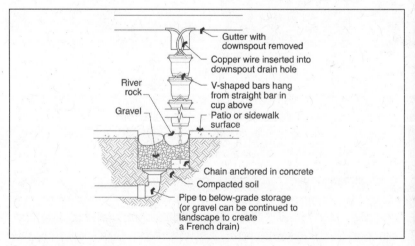

Gutter with downspout removed
Copper wire inserted into downspout drain hole
V-shaped bars hang from straight bar in cup above
Patio or sidewalk surface
River rock
Gravel
Chain anchored in concrete
Compacted soil
Pipe to below-grade storage (or gravel can be continued to landscape to create a French drain)

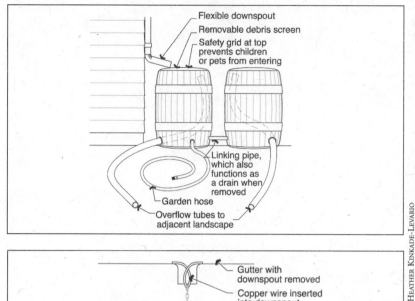

Flexible downspout
Removable debris screen
Safety grid at top prevents children or pets from entering

Linking pipe, which also functions as a drain when removed

Garden hose

Overflow tubes to adjacent landscape

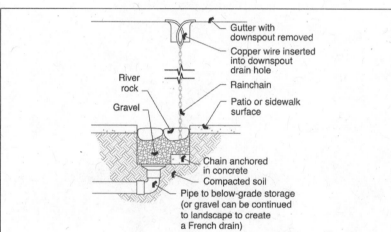

Gutter with downspout removed
Copper wire inserted into downspout drain hole

River rock
Gravel

Rainchain

Patio or sidewalk surface

Chain anchored in concrete
Compacted soil
Pipe to below-grade storage (or gravel can be continued to landscape to create a French drain)

LEFT: Linked rainbarrels
RIGHT: Rainbarrel

Rainchain ground connection

Rain cups

Rainchain/rain cup ground connection

Private residence which has an 18,000-gallon TimberTank in the back yard for rainwater collection

to remove and use the water just below the surface, is best to access the highest quality of water in the cistern. When high filtration is used or water quality directly from the tank is not an issue, a well pump may be used.

Water level gauges can be electronic for above- or below-grade tanks. Above-grade tanks have the option for simple devices. The Levitator is a storage tank level indicator that is on a pulley and counterweight system with a free hanging ball on the outside of the tank, adjacent to the wall of the tank, that rises or lowers with the level of the water inside the tank. The Liquidator is a tank level indicator that is similar to the Levatator, but the external level indicator is in a tube to protect it from wind and other elements. The Dipstik is a sliding pole mounted to the top of a tank that slides up as the water rises and slides down as the water lowers. There are other

Private residence which has an 8,800-gallon tank

TOP LEFT:
New Braunfels Utilities five 15,000-gallon tanks
TOP RIGHT:
Metal tank roof
MIDDLE RIGHT:
Metal tank in woods
BOTTOM LEFT:
Old metal rainwater tank
BOTTOM RIGHT:
Tanks above house

Heather Kinkade-Levario

Shawn Hatley, Blue Ridge

Left:
Corrugate metal
pipe cistern

Top Right:
Tanks under deck

Bottom Right:
Wooden Tank

Heather Kinkade-Levario

Rain Alert receiver in the
house with a small LCD read-
out panel that continually
shows the tank water level

Sandy Murdoch, Rain Harvesting Pty Ltd

Rain Alert transmitter
on tank

Sandy Murdoch, Rain Harvesting Pty Ltd

tank level indicators such as the Level Devil that are similar to the Liquidator, and equilibrium tubes that show water in a tube at the same height as the water in the tank. An additional product is a new tank level indicator that has been brought to the market by Rain Harvesting Pty Ltd out of Australia. It is called Rain Alert and is a combination transmitter (attached to the tank) and receiver (inside the house) that can function within a 650-foot range.

MAINTENANCE OF STORAGE SYSTEMS

1. Inspect all inlets and outlets before and after each rain event to remove blockages or repair broken parts. Clean any and all screens.

2. Inspect all access lids to ensure seals are tight enough to deter insects and animals.

3. Inspect above-grade tank sides for damage and leaks. Repair

any problem areas.

4. Check foundation or base for any settling or cracking, initially after each rain event, eventually on a yearly basis.

5. Check all seams for leaks.

6. For potable supplies, check water quality monthly.

7. Maintain mosquito control if mosquitoes are breeding.

8. Empty below-grade tanks periodically (every 3 to 5 years) to check for leaks, waterproofing damage, and any structural damage. Checking at the lowest storage point may also be efficient.

9. Check all pumps and other working equipment—such as alternative water supply on/off switch—every six months to guarantee working condition.

10. Maintain air gap if alternative water source is used to fill tanks or cisterns during dry periods.

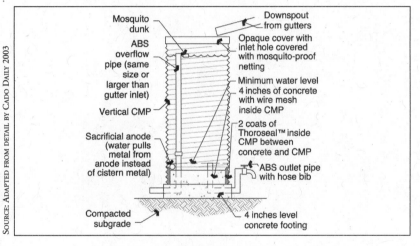

Vertical Corrugated metal pipe (CMP) cistern

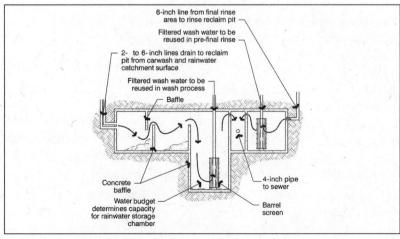

Carwash reclaim pit

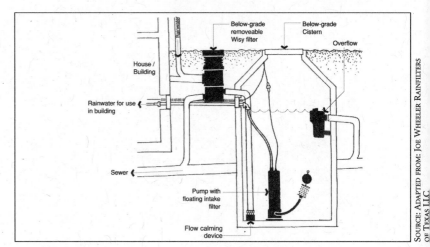

Cistern lid with vent to be secured and tight enough to keep out insects and animals, but also allow tank to vent

Connection to municipal water/ makeup water

To pump and pressure tank

Hole in pipe to prevent syphone effect

Overflow inlet (minimum 12 inches below municipal water services)

Downspout from gutters

Floating or stationary pump inlet

First-flush diversion device

Aerobic Zone

Drain valve or hose bib

Optional turbulence calming device to prevent remixing of sediment

Minimum water level 6 inches

Overflow to French drain or surface water drain (cover end with netting or wire mesh or flap valve to keep out insects and animals)

Anaerobic zone

Above-grade cistern

German cistern with WISY filter, submersible pump, and overflow/ multi siphon

Rainwater

House / Building

Below-grade removeable Wisy filter

Below-grade Cistern

Overflow

Rainwater for use in building

Sewer

Pump with floating intake filter

Flow calming device

SOURCE: ADAPTED FROM: JOE WHEELER RAINFILTERS OF TEXAS LLC

Potable Water Treatment Technologies

Collected rainwater can be purified for drinking water supplies. An initial water test must be conducted to evaluate harvested water content. As mentioned earlier, the rainwater content will be dependent on the catchment surface, gutter, and downspout materials. Below are typical water treatment technologies; additional steps and filters may be required for various systems.

Absorption: Carbon filters provide absorption.

Ultraviolet light: Ultraviolet light disinfects water by reducing the amount of heterotrophic bacteria present in the water.

Reverse osmosis: Water passes from a more concentrated solution to a more dilute solution through a semipermeable membrane. Most systems should incorporate a cyst and particulate pre- and post-filter in addition to the membrane.

Distiller: Water is heated to the boiling point and the water vapor is collected as it condenses, leaving many of the contaminants behind, particularly the heavy metals.

Ozone: Naturally occurring allotrope of oxygen has the highest oxidation potential of all available oxidants.

Inorganic and organic materials can be oxidized by ozone more rapidly and at lower residual concentrations than by other chemical means. Ozone is typically aspirated via high-efficiency injectors while the cistern water is circulated through a side-stream contacting system or through a bottom-of-cistern diffusion grid.

There are two styles of water treatment:

Point-of-entry system: Water is

HEATHER KINKADE-LEVARIO

Rainwater and other control systems mounted on wall inside the Eco Building, Phoenix, AZ

Various harvested rainwater purification processes

```
                    ┌──────────────────────┐
                    │   Catchment Area     │
                    └──────────────────────┘
                                │
                                ▼
                    ┌──────────────────────┐    ┌──────────────────────┐
                    │ First-flush /        │ ▶  │  Discharge Pollution │
                    │ Roof Washing         │    └──────────────────────┘
                    └──────────────────────┘
                                │
                                ▼
┌──────────────────────┐   ┌──────────────┐    ┌──────────────────────┐
│ Alternate Water      │ ▶ │   Storage    │ ▶  │      Overflow        │
│ Supply               │   └──────────────┘    └──────────────────────┘
│ (Need only as backup │
│ for rainwater        │
│ supplies)            │
└──────────────────────┘
```

Solar Distiller (Could be used instead of inline filtration)	Sediment Filter 5.0 Micron	Absolute Filter 1.0 Micron (NSF approved for cyst removal)
▼	▼	▼
Any additional filtration as needed per water test results.	Carbon Filter 0.5 Micron (NSF approved for cyst removal)	Carbon Filter 10.0 Micron
▼	▼	▼
Distribution	Ultraviolet or Ozone Disinfection	Ultraviolet Disinfection
	▼	▼
	Distribution	Distribution

HEATHER KINKADE-LEVARIO

treated prior to entering the building.

Point-of-use system: Water is treated for single use, such as kitchen or bathroom, and can include the following techniques:

- Bottled water
- Faucet mounted
- Countertop connected to sink faucet
- Plumbed to separate tap
- Pour-through products or gravity drip
- Counter-top manual fill

MAINTENANCE OF DRINKING WATER FILTRATION DEVICES

1. Test water quality frequently, every six months minimum.

2. Change filters more often than suggested in manufacturers' guidelines.

3. Check for leaks daily, or weekly at a minimum.

4. Ozone treatment of water stored in cisterns is an option for maintaining water quality.

5. All disinfection should occur after filters and prior to distribution, as filters can become infected.

Following is a sample water runoff worksheet, water budget worksheet, and a worksheet specific to potable uses only.

RainPC

The RainPC, made in the Netherlands, is a miniature water treatment plant that can provide household water security.

RainPC features

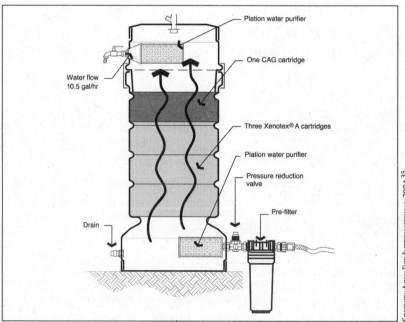

Platation water purifier

One CAG cartridge

Water flow 10.5 gal/hr

Three Xenotex® A cartridges

Platation water purifier

Pressure reduction valve

Pre-filter

Drain

SOURCE: AquaEst International 2004.[35]

RUNOFF WORKSHEET

Month	Area 1	Area 2	Area 3	Area 4	Total Monthly
January					
February					
March					
April					
May					
June					
July					
August					
September					
October					
November					
December					
Total Monthly Gallons					

Formula:

Area of Catchment Sq. Ft. (Length x Width)	X	Amount of Rainfall in Feet (Inches/12)	X	Catchment Efficiency (%)	X	Conversion Factor Gal./Cu. Ft. (7.48)	=	Runoff in Gallons (Total)

Runoff Worksheet (To be used in calculating runoff quantities)

NONPOTABLE WATER BUDGET WORKSHEET

Month	Total landscape irrigation requirement for established plants	Available runoff supply	Runoff minus landscape irrigation requirement	Excess runoff to storage (Not used each month)	Accumulative storage	Irrigation requirement from storage (Required to supplement irrigation requirement)	Irrigation requirement from municipal supply (No rainwater in storage tank)
January							
February							
March							
April							
May							
June							
July							
August							
September							
October							
November							
December							
Total Monthly Gallons							

POTABLE WATER BUDGET WORKSHEET

Step 1	Number of Users	2	
	Gallons per day/person	70	
	Gallons required per day	140	*(users x gpd/p =)*

| Step 2 | Days in residence/year. . . . . | 365 | |
| | Total water use per year . . . . | 51, 100 | *(gpd x days =)* |

Step 3	Rainfall (inches)	7	
	Water per sq. ft./inch of rain	0.623	
	Gallons water/sq. ft./year	4.36	*(rainfall x 0.623) =)*

Step 4	Total water needed per year	51, 100	
	Gallons water/sq. ft./year	4.36	
	sq. ft. collection area needed.	11,720	*(water needed/g sq. ft./year =)*

Step 5	Days storage required (varies)	90	
	Gallons required per day	140	
	Gallons of storage required	12,600	*(days stg x gpd =)*

System requirements for the above budget are as follows:
Rooftop catchment collection area required for this design based on rainfall in the surrounding area: 11,720 sq. ft.
Storage capacity required to supply system for periods without rain (summer): 12, 600 gallons

NOTE: The example shown here would require several catchment areas such as a house, patio, any sheds, and possibly any paved drives. It may not be possible to assemble an 11,720 sq. ft. catchment area, which means an alternate water source would be required for a potable system.

Potable Water Budget Worksheet (To
be used in calculating a water budget)

Stay-n-Play Pet Ranch rainwater system roof washer

Stay-n-Play Pet Ranch building

Impurities and contaminants are removed from the stored rainwater as it passes upward through the RainPC's five-stage purification process. The rainwater first flows through a pre-filter that takes out all particles larger than 5 microns. It then passes through a drum-cage containing ceramic spheres with silver colloids and then through three activated-mineral composite Xenotex-A cartridges, an activated carbon filter with silver particles, and finally a specially developed low-pressure MF membrane filter.

After passing through this compact unit, which requires only low gravity pressure to

Heather Kinkade-Levario

*Ultraviolet
light filter*

Pioneer Water Tanks - A BlueScope Water Company

Heather Kinkade-Levario

*LEFT (TOP TO BOTTOM):
A Pioneer Galaxy water
storage tank in California*

*Rainwater tank at
Wollongong Botanic Garden
in New South Wales, AU*

RIGHT (TOP TO BOTTOM):

Tank painted like a turtle

Tank painted like a ladybug

Pioneer Water Tanks - A BlueScope Water Company

Heather Kinkade-Levario

function, the water is ready to drink. A RainPC should be placed at an elevation lower than the cistern or the cistern water could be pumped to an elevation higher than the RainPC to allow gravity to push the rainwater through the unit.

TECHNICAL DATA
Dimensions
Height: 32 inches
Diameter body: 12.4 inches
Diameter assembled: maximum 18.8 inches

Weight
Unit assembled, including cartridges: 55 lbs
Xenotex-A cartridge: 6.6 lbs
CAG cartridge: 4.4 lbs

Materials
PVC house bottom, body, and top
Steel clamp ring
Nickelbrass faucet

Brass water meter

Pressure Reduction Valve
For maximum 6 bar to 0.2 bar

Connections
Drinking water outlet valve, diameter $^1/_2$ inch
Rainwater inlet, diameter $^1/_2$ inch
Drain outlet, diameter $^1/_2$ inch
Water meter outlet, diameter $^3/_4$ inch

Costs
The cost of a rainwater harvesting system varies greatly depending on the extent of the system. Some costs of a system

VARIOUS STORAGE TANKS AND AVERAGE COSTS PER BUILDING MATERIAL

Material	Estimated Cost	Typical Size
Barrel (Plastic Rain, wooden whiskey, or metal)	Free, to $300 per barrel	200 – 500 gallons
Concrete or Ferro-Cement (Precast concrete tanks)	$0.35 up to $1.50 per gallon	Any
Fiberglass	$0.50 to $2.00 per gallon	500 – 20,000 gallons
Metal (Corrugated with liner, galvanized steel)	$0.30 to $2.79 per gallon	150 – 104,000 gallons
Polyethylene	$0.50 to $1.90 per gallon	210 – 5,000 gallons
Polypropylene	$0.35 to $1.00 per gallon	290 – 20,000 gallons
Welded steel (Bolted stainless steel)	$0.80 to $4.00 per gallon	1,000 – 1 million gallons
Wooden (Treated wood with liners)	$0.88 to $2.06 per gallon	700 – 2 million gallons
Stone	Very expensive; up to $1.00 per square foot of tank surface area	Any
Crates: Invisible Structures RainStore 3	$8.00 per cubic foot	Any
Crates: Atlantis	$4.84 to $5.15 per cubic foot	Any

The 2-gallon pressure tank used for rainwater in bathroom and for evaporative coolers

HEATHER KINKADE-LEVARIO

LEFT (TOP TO BOTTOM):
Australian Slimline tank; note the leaf filter basket and the first-flush stand pipe on the downspout, and rainwater piped back into the house for laundry and flushing toilets

A 2,000-liter residential rainwater tank with a stand pipe and leaf catcher

RIGHT (TOP TO BOTTOM): Private residential Pioneer Galaxy water storage tank in Western Australia

Three black poly water storage tanks, 2,340 gallons each

should be assumed building costs such as gutters on residential homes or gutters and downspouts on commercial buildings. Retrofitting a building is always more expensive than building the components into the original design. Double plumbing for flushing toilets or washing clothes with rainwater should be an option with original designs as it may be too costly to retrofit a building for this option. If a building is in a remote location with no municipal supply or well available, the costs may be less of an issue.

The single most expense in a system is the storage tank or cistern and price is based on the quantity of water to be stored and the material the storage is made from. The intended use may dictate the material of the storage tank. Storage units can range in price from a low $0.30 per gallon to a high of $4.00 per gallon.[36]

Gutters used for water collection should be made from vinyl, plastic, aluminum, or galvalume. The gutters made from these materials can range in price from $0.30 per lineal foot to $12.00 per lineal foot.

Vertical and horizontal box roof washers can range in price from $460 to $1,000.

Pre-filters can range in price from $50 each to $80 for larger systems.

Pressure tanks range in price from $200 to $1,000.

Pumps range in size and price from a 1-horsepower

Grundfos at $585 to a $3/4$-horse-power Gould at $585 to a 1-horse power Gould at $635.

Filters can be cartridge filter sets (includes 5 micron and 3 micron charcoal) at $100; one micron filters at $265; reverse-osmosis filters at $400 to $1,500; UV filters at $300 to $1,000 with replacement bulbs costing $80 to $100; ozone disinfection systems at $700 to $2,600; and chlorine disinfection systems at a manual cost of $1 per dose or $600 to $3,000 for an automatic system. Floating cistern filters cost approximately $265.

Prices quoted are approximate 2006 costs and were price estimates from:

Texas Guide to Rainwater Harvesting; braewater.com; specallproducts.com; invisiblestructures.com; plasticstoragetanks.com;

rainwatercollection.com; and rainwatermanagement.com.

An installed rainwater harvesting system providing all six components including potable water suited for a four-person household may cost as much as $22,000.[37] A commercial project could install a rainwater harvesting system for less if underground flood retention is proposed and drywells are eliminated. Although there are many passive rainwater techniques that cost very little—even a barrel can be used for rainwater collection—there is a wide range of costs, depending on an owner's commitment to water conservation. Cost-recovery times for a sophisticated residential rainwater harvesting system in other parts of the modern world have been estimated to be around 16 years.[38]

Examples of Handmade Tanks

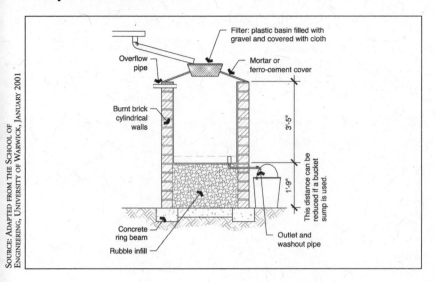

Source: Adapted from the School of Engineering, University of Warwick, January 2001

Filter: plastic basin filled with gravel and covered with cloth

Overflow pipe

Mortar or ferro-cement cover

Burnt brick cylindrical walls

3'-5"

This distance can be reduced if a bucket sump is used.

1'-9"

Concrete ring beam

Rubble infill

Outlet and washout pipe

Brick jar from Uganda

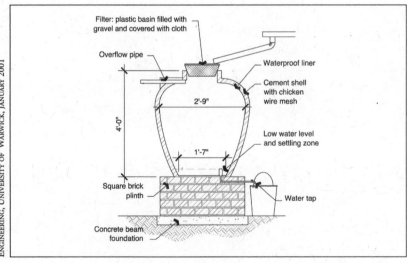

Ferro-cement jar from Uganda

Source: Adapted from the School of Engineering, University of Warwick, January 2001

Filter: plastic basin filled with gravel and covered with cloth

Overflow pipe

Waterproof liner

Cement shell with chicken wire mesh

2'-9"

4'-0"

Low water level and settling zone

1'-7"

Square brick plinth

Water tap

Concrete beam foundation

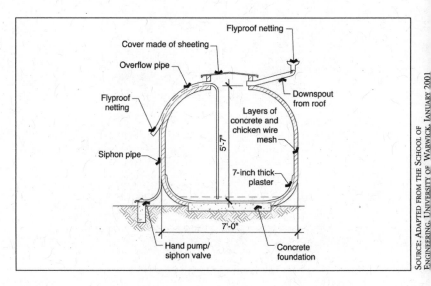

Underground brick dome tank from Sri Lanka

Downspout from roof

Three coats of plaster similar to inside

Cloth for filtering water

Aluminum sheet cover with opening

Hand pump

Ground level

Flyproof netting

Dome built with brick in cement sand mortar

Overflow pipe

Internal plaster 7'-6"

4'-0"

1-inch diameter suction pipe

Concrete floor

Foot valve

Brick wall in cement sand mortar

Pumpkin tank from Sri Lanka

Flyproof netting

Cover made of sheeting

Overflow pipe

Flyproof netting

Siphon pipe

Downspout from roof

Layers of concrete and chicken wire mesh

5'-7"

7-inch thick plaster

7'-0"

Hand pump/siphon valve

Concrete foundation

SOURCE: ADAPTED FROM THE SCHOOL OF ENGINEERING, UNIVERSITY OF WARWICK, JANUARY 2001

SOURCE: ADAPTED FROM THE SCHOOL OF ENGINEERING, UNIVERSITY OF WARWICK, JANUARY 2001

Equipment for an Active Rainwater Catchment Syste

5 Case Studies

> *When the well is dry, we learn the worth of water.*
>
> — Ben Franklin

THE FOLLOWING is a collection of case studies that will provide the understanding to attain dreams— dreams of catching and reusing water that is provided to a site through natural or artificial means. There are several sections to this collection starting with landscape infiltration and continuing through individual private rooftop catchment systems to multiple building systems that support residential subdivisions.

Commercial rooftop rainwater catchment systems, industrial rooftop rainwater catchment systems, water catchment systems for schools of all levels, parks, and interpretive center systems, and large scale municipal systems are provided for reference and further study.

Alternate water systems that include fog collection, cooling tower blowdown water collection, air conditioning condensate water collection, and greywater

A private residential 35,000 gallon Pioneer Galaxy water storage tank used for rainwater collection in the hill country of Texas

Jack Hall, Spec-All Products, Inc.

*Two eastern red
cedar wood tanks
outside a retail building*

collection are provided to demonstrate the potential for saving purified municipal water. Rainwater catchment for wildlife is also provided as an example of how water can be provided to locations that do not have a naturally accumulated water source.

Landscape Infiltration

OREGON CONVENTION CENTER—PORTLAND, OREGON

Location:	Portland, Oregon
Type of system:	Passive rooftop for infiltration
Year installed:	2003
Annual rainfall:	Approx. 52 inches
Catchment area:	Rooftop – 5.5-acres
Containment:	None
Annual quantity collected:	Approx. 6.9 million gallons
Water usage:	Rain garden infiltration
Equipment involved:	Pumps – None Cistern level controls – None Pressure tank – None Filters – Natural plants and soil
Contact:	Landscape Architect: Mayer/ Reed, Portland, Oregon www.mayerreed.com

The Oregon Convention Center stormwater garden is located on the south side of the building between the building and the adjacent road. The 5.5-acre roof drains via downspouts in four locations along the linear stepped garden. While most of Portland's stormwater drains into the city's sewer system, this site was granted a direct pipe to the adjacent Willamette River. However, instead of dumping the potentially polluted site water directly into the river, the project Landscape Architect decided to infiltrate the runoff water, and allow the plants and soil to filter pollutants and maintain water quality levels.

The rain garden mimics a stream flowing through the site. The rainwater travels through a series of shallow, cascading, ungrouted rock-lined pools. Each pool is separated by low rock weirs to allow the water standing and infiltrating time. The weirs also slow the water allowing any sediment to drop out before continuing on downstream. Once a pool is full the rainwater spills over the weir and drops about 18 inches into the next pool. This stream travels 318 feet, and averages about 6 feet wide. The dramatic garden is made by using a variety of flat flagstone, small river rock, angular retaining wall stones, and columnar basalt pieces. The channel edge against the road is reinforced with a steel plate to eliminate erosion potential and to maintain structural stability. The soils underlying the rock channel are a mixture of sand and Troutdale formation soil. The soils allow most of the slow rains to infiltrate quickly.

The rain garden channel ends in a detention pond that also receives runoff from a 205-foot vegetated swale that captures runoff from the truck loading area. In the rare occasions the pond fills, there is a 30-inch public storm drain pipe installed. The plants are obviously enjoying the extra drink, as they are very lush.

HEATHER KINKADE-LEVARIO

Entry to the Oregon Convention Center

LEFT:
Downspout from building to rain garden
RIGHT:
Downspout to a less-vegetated channel

HEATHER KINKADE-LEVARIO

HEATHER KINKADE-LEVARIO

First downspout in the system

Signage recognizing the rain gardens

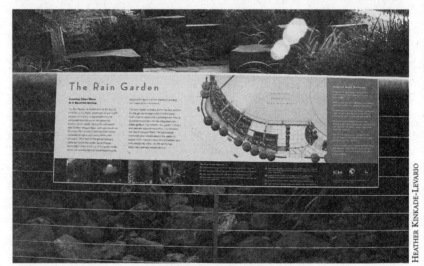

View of the rain gardens from the southwest

HEATHER KINKADE-LEVARIO

HEATHER KINKADE-LEVARIO

Pedestrian crossings with signage allow visitors to understand the rock channel and the natural cycle taking place.

Details of this system can be found in the September 2004 edition of *Landscape Architecture* magazine, page 64.

SEATTLE NATURAL DRAINAGE SYSTEM—SEATTLE PUBLIC UTILITIES

Seattle's creeks carry pollution from roadways, streets, and parking lots to the Puget Sound, impacting the food chain that supports fish and other wildlife in the area. The fish that are impacted by this pollution—including salmon and steelhead trout—are a symbol of the northwest, requiring preservation. Therefore, a new solution for the rainwater that carries these pollutants was needed. The City of Seattle approved an initial planning grant to find a solution, and the resulting new concept is now known as the Seattle Public Utilities Natural Drainage System.

The concept was initially implemented in a northwest Seattle neighborhood that had inadequate stormwater manage-

ment. It was initiated in an innovative study to determine the potential for cleanup of the pollutants carried by the stormwater runoff. By 2004 the project had succeeded well beyond the initial expectations and has now been implemented in five new smaller projects and one larger project covering fifteen city blocks in northwest Seattle's Piper's Creek watershed.

This new approach meets multiple goals including helping to manage flooding in neighborhoods; improving appearance and function of streets; providing responsible stewardship of the environment; and helping the City to meet local, state, and national environmental regulations. The system utilizes soil and plants to substantially

Location:	Seattle, Washington
Type of system:	Passive rooftop and ground level for infiltration
Year installed:	2002
Annual rainfall:	Approx. 52 inches
Catchment area:	Four block area, 21 acres
Containment:	None
Annual quantity collected:	Unknown
Water usage:	Rain garden infiltration
Equipment involved:	Pumps — None Cistern level controls — None Pressure tank — None Filters — Natural plants and soil
Contact:	Seattle Public Utilities www.ci.seattle.wa.us.

Heather Kinkade-Levario

Stepped cascade rain gardens at initial completion

Younger rain garden where vegetation has not reach maturity; this is a cascade garden

Heather Kinkade-Levario

Cascade rain garden

Heather Kinkade-Levario

Heather Kinkade-Levario

Heather Kinkade-Levario

Heather Kinkade-Levario

Heather Kinkade-Levario

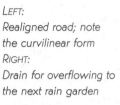

LEFT:
Realigned road; note
the curvilinear form
RIGHT:
Drain for overflowing to
the next rain garden

LEFT:
Drain pipe emptying
into a rain garden
RIGHT:
Rain garden between
two drives; this is a rain
garden running with the
contours of the land

Sidewalk between
the residential lot and
the natural drainage
system rain gardens

Heather Kinkade-Levario

decrease runoff by allowing it to infiltrate to natural subsurface hydrologic systems and reduce pollutants as the water infiltrates through the soil. The system allows nature to restore and conduct the processes it was intended to do.

This approach is completed by narrowing roads and constructing rain gardens or infiltration cells along the side of the road. These open-space areas left from narrowing of the roads are then designed with plants and highly permeable soils. The gardens are interlinked to create a network of vegetated swales and "cascades" that absorb the stormwater. The swales run with the contours, and drain into the cascades that cut and step down the contours of the development.

The City of Seattle has determined that in addition to the environmental benefits the system is providing it is also a more cost effective way to treat stormwater than the traditional approaches.[39] Treating the stormwater where it falls has reduced the need to build and maintain costly treatment pipes and holding facilities. Seattle Public Utilites estimates the Natural Drainage System costs 25 percent less than tra-ditional roadways and storm drain facilities.[40]

Details of this system can be found at Carkeek Cascade NW 110th St. on the Seattle Public Utilities web page, www.seattle.gov/util/services/ (search: Carkeek Cascade).

Residential: Single-Family and Multi-Family Rainwater Harvesting Systems

COLE RESIDENCE—SAN JUAN ISLANDS

Location:	Friday Harbor, Washington
Type of system:	Active rooftop
Year installed:	2005
Annual rainfall:	Approx. 42 inches
Catchment area:	Rooftop – 5,000 square feet
Containment:	Above-grade 30,000-gallon metal tank and one 240-gallon ball tank for collecting from all down spouts prior to gravity feed to tank
Annual quantity collected:	Approx. 117,810 gallons
Water usage:	Potable water supply
Equipment involved:	Pumps – Grundfos 3-horsepower pump Cistern level controls – Yes Pressure tank – 60 gallon Filters – UV, 5 and 1 micron, and 3-micron charcoal filter
Contact:	Design and installation by Tim Pope, Friday Harbor, Washington water@interisland.net

The Cole Residence is in a wooded area on the San Juan Islands. The islands in this part of the United States are having problems with their ground water quality as the saltwater has begun to intrude into the supply, and in the area of the Cole Residence there are also problems with barium in the groundwater. In an effort to eliminate all polluted water the family has implemented a rainwater catchment system to provide all potable water. The remote location of the home also requires a fire-fighting water supply that the local fire and emergency trucks can hook into when needed.

The home is located 45 feet above the water storage tank. The rainwater is initially directed to a ball tank that filters the

Equipment room with pump and filters

LEFT:
Pressure tank for
the system
RIGHT:
Tank with the fire
hose connection

rainwater through gravel in the bottom of the tank. The ball tank also works as a manifold for directing water from the multiple drain pipes to a gravity-fed pipe that leads into—from the bottom—the main storage tank situated below the home.

The main storage tank is fitted with two withdrawing pipes; the first is a vertical pipe that reaches to the tank floor. This pipe remains as a fire-pump apparatus for emergency use. The second pipe enters through the tank floor and is attached to a 3-horsepower pump and a 60-gallon pressure buffer tank, which returns to feed the home above.

The metal tank is lined with a 35-mm polypropylene material that includes a nylon mesh layer to add strength. The liner sits on a tank floor of bricks set in sand. It reaches up the walls of the metal tank and is attached at the top of the tank, which is enclosed with a metal roof.

KEARNEY RESIDENCE—CATALINA MOUNTAINS

Located in the foothills of the Catalina Mountains north of Tucson, the Kearney Residence displays an excellent use of slope to incorporate a rainwater cistern. The system was installed in 1990 when the existing home was remodeled. Because the home site is fairly steep, the cistern top could be located at an elevation that permitted its use as a patio.

The site-constructed integral concrete block cistern uses gravity to feed a hose bibb at its base. No first-flush device is installed prior to the cistern. Water is only collected from the rooftop, where very little debris accumulates. A hand-held hose is used to irrigate the desert landscape material. The site is augmented with swales that lead to planting basins, and downspouts that are directed to adjacent planters.

Integral cistern with landscape planter below

Patio above cistern; metal lid on surface is the cistern access

HEATHER KINKADE-LEVARIO

HEATHER KINKADE-LEVARIO

Location: Tucson, Arizona

Type of system:	Active rooftop
Year installed:	1990
Annual rainfall:	11.4 inches in the foothills
Catchment area:	Rooftop – 4,000 square feet
Containment:	One 7,000-gallon concrete block tank with stone veneer
Annual quantity collected:	24,800 gallons
Water usage:	Irrigation, nonpotable
Equipment involved:	Pumps – None Cistern level controls – Visual Pressure tank – None Filters – None
Contact:	Richard Brittain, University of Arizona Tucson, Arizona www.architecture.arizona.edu/ people.asp?topic=faculty

HEATHER KINKADE-LEVARIO

Passive water collection swale that leads to the landscape basin

CAMINO BLANCA—CAMINO CRUZ BLANCA ROAD

The Camino Blanca Residence is located on a hillside of Santa Fe, New Mexico. The residence roof drains in multiple directions, requiring thirteen catch basins to collect all the roof runoff water. All the captured water drains, by gravity, to three 2,000-gallon Darco tanks. The tanks are made of polyethylene and can be connected to each other for modular, unlimited water storage capacity. The Darco tanks connect at the ends, and are nicknamed "OcTanks" due to the eight-sided internal rib design that gives the tank its strength and rigidity when buried.

These tanks can withstand automotive and water-truck loading. They are typically buried at a 3-foot depth, and equipped with manway risers and vents. The tanks can be made from virgin polyethylene resin, which is NSF listed and complies with the FDA 21 to allow potable water systems. A shallow basin is located next to the tanks for overflow purposes. The pump for this residence is a Grundfos jet pump that supplies the irrigation-line pressure.

Location: Santa Fe, New Mexico	
Type of system:	Active rooftop
Year installed:	2005
Annual rainfall:	Average 14.3 inches
Catchment area:	Rooftop – 5,475 square feet
Containment:	Below-grade, three 2,000 gallons each
Annual quantity collected:	Approx. 40,331 gallons
Water usage:	Irrigation water supply
Equipment involved:	Pumps – Grundfos MO3-45 jet pump, Hydromatic series 20 submersible pump Cistern level controls – Digital water quality indicating system Pressure tank – Not available Filters – Inline conveyance filter
Contact:	A Desert Rain System by The Hydros Group Santa Fe, New Mexico www.thehydrosgroup.com

SOURCE: ADAPTED FROM THE THE HYDROS GROUP DESIGN

The site plan for the project shows the catch basins and pipes for collecting the rooftop rainwater and the lines to the Darco tanks; the irrigation service is also shown exiting the tanks

RANCHO SAN MARCOS—CHAPMAN COMPANIES

Rancho San Marcos is a single-family home that was constructed to demonstrate innovative technologies. The Partnership for Advancing Technologies in Housing (PATH), managed and supported by the US Department of

Type of system:	Active rooftop
Year installed:	2000
Annual rainfall:	10-12 inches
Catchment area:	Rooftop – 2,300 square feet
Containment:	Below-grade, one 1,200-gallon polypropylene tank for rainwater and a 55-gallon package greywater system called GURU or Greywater Universal Reclamation Unit, made by Earthstar Energy Systems
Annual quantity collected:	Approx. 15,484 gallons of rainwater and approx. 18,000 gallons grey water collected, approx. 27 gallons per day
Water usage:	Landscape irrigation water supply
Equipment involved:	Pumps – 1.5 horsepower for the rainwater system. Cistern level controls – Manual. Pressure tank – None. Filters – Only on the pump intake of the rainwater pump. The greywater system uses a sand filter.
Costs of system:	$3,000 per home for the rainwater system and $2,500 per home for the extra greywater pipes and GURU system.
Contact:	Design and installation by Chapman Companies, Santa Fe, New Mexico, www.chapmandcompanies.com Rainwater and greywater system components provided by Jade Mountain, Inc. www.jademountain.com (now Gaiam/RealGoods)

Housing and Urban Development (HUD), conducted the field evaluation for the use of greywater and rainwater collection systems for the Rancho San Marcos home. The research was conducted due to the water shortages in the area.

The greywater system chosen was a package system that included a 12-gallon storage (sometimes called surge) tank connected to a centrifugal pump and a sand filter with self-cleaning capabilities. The greywater system was purchased from Jade Mountain, Inc. of Boulder, Colorado and was connected to the drainpipes from the bathroom sinks, showers, and

TOP: Front view of the home
BOTTOM: Greywater and rainwater equipment access lids

Chapman Homes

Chapman Homes

Greywater and rain-water pump and equipment in sump

Greywater sump schematic

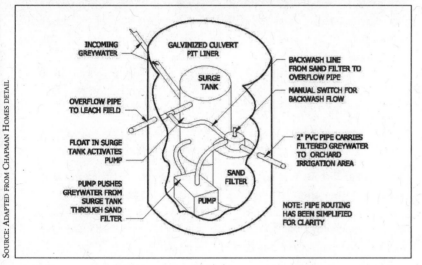

INCOMING GREYWATER

GALVINIZED CULVERT PIT LINER

SURGE TANK

BACKWASH LINE FROM SAND FILTER TO OVERFLOW PIPE

MANUAL SWITCH FOR BACKWASH FLOW

OVERFLOW PIPE TO LEACH FIELD

FLOAT IN SURGE TANK ACTIVATES PUMP

2" PVC PIPE CARRIES FILTERED GREYWATER TO ORCHARD IRRIGATION AREA

PUMP PUSHES GREYWATER FROM SURGE TANK THROUGH SAND FILTER

SAND FILTER

PUMP

NOTE: PIPE ROUTING HAS BEEN SIMPLIFIED FOR CLARITY

bathtubs. The package system comes ready to hook up to the house drainpipes and is designed to turn on the self-priming centrifugal Hayward Power-Flo II, 15-amp, 115 volt, 3/4-horsepower pump when the surge tank fills to pump the greywater through the attached sand filter.

The pump does have a strainer filter on the suction side of the line that needs to be cleaned monthly. Once the water is collected and filtered it is delivered to the site's six orna-mental fruit trees through a 2-inch pipe. The sand filter is 0.45-0.55 mm. pool filter sand, and filters out dirt, hair, grease, and other particles. Periodically the sand filter must be back-washed to remove the accumulated debris. A 3-way diverter valve allows the greywa-ter to be diverted back to the house sewer system for back-washing or if the greywater system needs repair or cleaning.

The roof top rainwater is

collected via gutters and downspouts to a 1,220-gallon plastic tank. The buried tank has a 2-foot diameter access hatch with a cover at grade level. An overflow system consisting of a 6-inch perforated pipe runs to the orchard. A solenoid valve and float switch control the backup system that is a line from the site's well, which fills the tank when the collected rainwater is exhausted. The switch fills the tank with the daily irrigation requirements of 200 gallons of water, leaving approximately 1,000 gallons of capacity for rainwater that may be collected.

A 1.5-horsepower pump draws the rainwater out of the tank into an irrigation system that waters a rear-yard lawn and several shrubs as well as shrub in the front yard.

The landscape irrigation needs are estimated at 150 to 200 gallons daily. By using both the greywater and rainwater systems, Chapman Companies was able to provide an extra water supply of approximately 14,179 gallons, allowing certain shrubs and plants, which are not normally provided in the builder's landscape package, to be included.

SINGLE-FAMILY QUADPLEX—TUCSON BARRIO REDEVELOPMENT AREA

Location:	Tucson, Arizona
Type of system:	Active rooftop
Year installed:	2001
Annual rainfall:	12 inches
Catchment area:	Rooftop — 2,000 square feet
Containment:	Above-grade, three 370-gallon corrugated metal cisterns
Annual quantity collected:	Approx. 40,392 gallons for all three cisterns
Water usage:	Landscape irrigation
Equipment involved:	Pumps — Gravity Cistern level controls — Visual Pressure tank — None Filters — None
Contact:	Design and installation by Dave Taggett, Tucson, Arizona. (No website address available)

View of courtyard and cisterns prior to carport completion

These four homes are not attached other than by fencing. The area between the homes was divided into four courtyards. Each courtyard has three cisterns, two at the end of the individual carport and one on the side of the home. The rainwater gravity-feeds into the cisterns that are 7 feet tall and

HEATHER KINKADE-LEVARIO

View of the four-home
quadplex and carports
from the street after
carport completion

One tank on the main
patio with two in the
adjacent yard. This
homeowner opted to
remove one of the
cisterns at the end of
their carport

Two tanks in adjacent
courtyard at the end of
the carport

HEATHER KINKADE-LEVARIO

HEATHER KINKADE-LEVARIO

approximately 3 feet in diameter, holding approximately 370 gallons of water.

The cisterns are made from corrugated metal pipes that have been turned on end to create tanks. The housing architecture fits well with the corrugated metal pipe cisterns and they add a touch of "artsy" look to the complex. The systems are entirely gravity feed; no filters or pumps are used, and the collected water is only used for a gravity feed landscape irrigation system.

CASA RUFINA—APARTMENT COMPLEX

*This site plan shows
a typical building
layout with catch
basins and lines to
the Darco tanks*

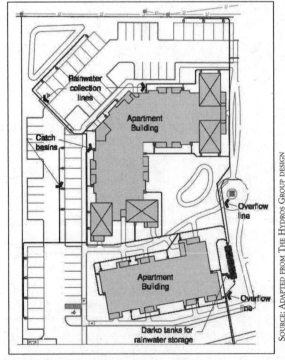

Rainwater
collection
lines

Apartment
Building

Catch
basins

Overflow
line

Apartment
Building

Overflow
line

Darko tanks for
rainwater storage

SOURCE: ADAPTED FROM THE HYDROS GROUP DESIGN

Casa Rufina is an apartment complex located in Santa Fe, New Mexico with seven residential buildings and a clubhouse. The total roof area collected from is approximately 92,260 sq. ft., which includes catchment from all the buildings as well as covered parking areas. The roof runoff is directed to four different groups of five Darco tanks. Each group of Darco tanks holds a total of 10,000 gallons.

Two of the tanks are designed to overflow to the others if they reach maximum capacity; this insures that all rainwater is captured and not lost. Each tank system supplies pressurized water to its own irri-

Location:	Santa Fe, New Mexico
Type of system:	Active rooftop
Year installed:	2005
Annual rainfall:	12-14 inches
Catchment area:	Rooftop — 92,260 square feet
Containment:	Below-grade, four 10,000-gallon modules of Darco tanks
Annual quantity collected:	699,873 gallons
Water usage:	Landscape irrigation
Equipment involved:	Pumps — Hydromatic HE-20 submersible Cistern level controls — Digital water-quality indicating system Pressure tank — Not available Filters — Graf Universal large scale filter system
Contact:	A Desert Rain System by The Hydros Group www.thehydrosgroup.com

gation system that provides water for that specific area or group of apartments. This system also has the DRS Switching System, a specialty system designed by the Hydros Group specifically for switching water supplies in a tank. The rainwater catchment system was also designed to take on additional roof catchment water when the next expansion is built.

The pump system is a Hydromatic HE-20 Submersible system. The filter is a Graf Universal large scale filter system that filters 100 percent of the water conveyed to the cisterns.

Residential Subdivisions: Rainwater Harvesting Systems

RANCHO VIEJO—SUNCOR DEVELOPMENT

Rancho Viejo is a 10,600-acre SunCor Development located south of Santa Fe, New Mexico. Due to high water-impact fees and the potential to maximize the number of units, rainwater harvesting systems were proposed to extend the water allocation provided to the development. Other water conservation measures were implemented including low-flow fixtures, prohibiting swimming pools, and implementing xeriscape landscapes. Irrigated areas were also limited to 1,000 square feet.

The rainwater is directed as it splashes down to the ground from the home's canales through cobble-filled catch basins with non-permeable liners to pipes that lead to the underground storage tank. Each system costs between $5,500 and $6,900. Each home system collects its own rainwater for that specific home's use. The average water usage per unit in 2001 was 58,600 gallons, and with the implementation of these rainwater systems the average unit water usage is estimated to drop to 29,300 gallons. SunCor now builds approximately 140 new homes yearly, each with a rainwater harvesting system.

Location:	Santa Fe, New Mexico
Type of system:	Active rooftop
Year installed:	2003
Annual rainfall:	Approx. 13 inches
Catchment area:	Rooftop — Approx. 2,500 square feet
Containment:	Below grade, one 600- or 1,200-gallon polypropylene tank
Annual quantity collected:	Approx. 18,513 gallons
Water usage:	Landscape irrigation water supply
Equipment involved:	Pumps — 1-horsepower Grundfos MQ-35 Cistern level controls — Manual Pressure tank — None Filters — Cobbles
Contact:	Design and installation by Aqua Harvest, Santa Fe, New Mexico www.aquaharvest.com www.ranchoviejo.com

Rancho Viejo entry signage

Bobcat loader delivering and placing a cistern

LEFT: Cistern located in hole with pipes in place
RIGHT: One recently placed and connected 1,200-gallon cistern

*Dual cisterns
being connected
to drainpipes*

*BOTTOM: A typical log
home in a western log
home subdivision*

WILKES COUNTY LOG HOME SUBDIVISION—HOME WATER SUPPLY FOR 250 LOG HOMES

The Wilkes County Log Home Development is a project currently under construction. When completed, the project will have 250 log homes with six different designs, four condo buildings with five condo units per building, and a clubhouse and pool. The rainwater catchment systems are the primary water supply for each home.

Each system captures rainwater from a 3,200 square foot metal roof, and is estimated to cost approximately $10,000 per unit. The designs will be integral to the design of the log homes.

The water enters the tanks through a first-flush system of a vortex fine filter to remove leaves and debris, and a smoothing inlet to prevent stirring up of

Location:	Wilkes County, North Carolina
Type of system:	Active rooftop
Year installed:	2006
Annual rainfall:	Average 51.5 inches
Catchment area:	Rooftop — Two-hundred fifty homes, each with 3,200 square foot catchment area
Containment:	Above- and below-grade each home, 5,000-gallon storage in two poly tanks
Annual quantity collected:	Approx. 144,401 gallons per home
Water usage:	Potable water supply
Equipment involved:	Pumps — 1-horsepower submersible pump, and a booster pump in the house Cistern level controls — Float switch Pressure tank — Not available Filters — First-flush, and tank filtration is a WISY floating filter in the tank, UV light, one sediment filter, and a carbon filter
Contact:	Rainwater Management Solutions, Salem, Virginia www.rainwatermanagement.com

Typical log home in a remote area

HEATHER KINKADE-LEVARIO

sediment that may settle in the bottom of the tanks. Each rain-water system will have two linked 2,500-gallon poly tanks.

The water in the tanks is retrieved with a normal switch-suction, submersible multiple-stage pressure pump. The pump is fitted with a floating filter intake system and a float switch to turn off the pump if water levels go below the minimum. The tanks are insulated for the cold weather experienced in the area, and have a pneumatic level indicator to display the water level.

Location:	Tesuque, New Mexico
Type of system:	Active rooftop
Year installed:	2006
Annual rainfall:	Average 13 inches
Catchment area:	Rooftop — Total unavailable, includes resort building and 50 cabin buildings
Containment:	Below-grade Atlantis D-Raintank system, 160,000 gallons
Annual quantity collected:	Unavailable
Water usage:	Landscape irrigation
Equipment involved:	Pumps — Hydromatic HE-20 submersible pump Cistern level controls — Digital water-quality indicating system Pressure tank — Not available Filters — Graf Universal large scale filter system
Contact:	A Desert Rain System by The Hydro Group, Santa Fe, New Mexico www.thehydrosgroup.com www.rancho-encantado.com

RANCHO ENCANTADO—RESORT AND CABINS

Rancho Encantado has quite a long history. Current history starts with the following excerpt from the resort's web site:

> In 1967, Betty Egan, a widow from Cleveland, Ohio with children in tow, found the ranch and immediately fell in love with the setting and the dream of a new life. In 1968, she re-christened the property Rancho Encantado or Enchanted Ranch, and opened the doors to guests once again. Her familial sense of hospitality quickly became legend. She had created a world-class resort with the casual ambiance of a ranch, all aspects reflecting her strong sense of the way things ought to be.

> Over the years the legend of Rancho Encantado grew as Betty's dedication to her special brand of hospitality attracted scores of famous guests including Prince Rainier and Princess Grace of Monaco and family, Princess Anne, The Dalai Lama, Maria Callas, Henry Fonda, Jimmy Stewart, John Wayne, and Frank Capra, among others.

> The sense of hospitality

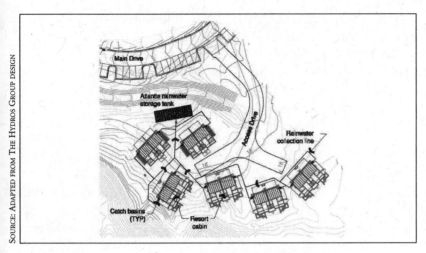

This site plan shows a typical cabin cluster, how the Atlantis tanks are located, and how the rainwater pipes connect the downspouts to the tanks

Atlantis rainwater storage tank schematic

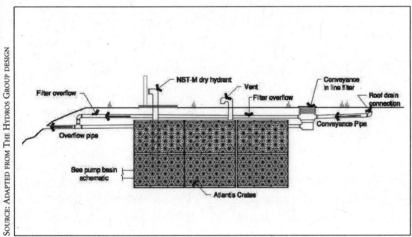

Atlantis pump basin schematic

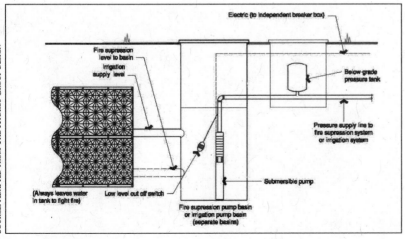

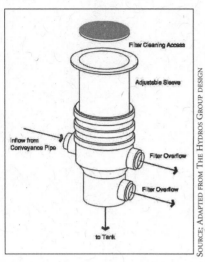

SOURCE: ADAPTED FROM THE HYDROS GROUP DESIGN

Convenience filter schematic

that Betty Egan created here will live on. She welcomed her guests to Rancho as she would to her home; this spirit is at the heart of the new Rancho Encantado. We continue to honor her and her spirit as we move forward.

Today the luxury resort, Rancho Encantado, located in Tesuque, New Mexico, has a rainwater catchment system. The system involves the multitude of guest cabin clusters conveying water to a tank system specific to the individual cabin cluster. The total volume stored is 160,000 gallons. Water is also captured from the pool deck area as well as the courtyards within the structures. Each of the catchment systems ties into a DRS Switching System (a system designed by The Hydros Group; it uses no electricity and has no moving parts). The pumps are Hydromatic HE-20 Submersible Systems and the filters are Graf Universal large scale filter systems that filter 100 percent of the water conveyed to the cistern systems.

CLUB CASITAS DE LAS CAMPANAS—LUXURY GOLF COURSE DEVELOPMENT

The Club Casitas de Las Campanas is a portion of the larger Las Campanas luxury golf course development on 4,800 acres located in Santa Fe, New Mexico. Las Campanas has two 18-hole world-class Jack Nicklaus Signature golf cours-es—the Sunrise and the Sunset. In addition to the golf courses, there is a spa and tennis center with six tennis courts, indoor and outdoor pools, and a gym. The community is surrounded by more than 66,000 acres of BLM land providing vistas, land

This site plan shows a typical casita cluster and how the Darco tanks are located, as well as how the rainwater pipes connect the downspouts and catch basins to the tanks.

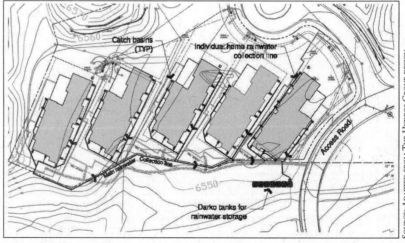

SOURCE: ADAPTED FROM THE HYDROS GROUP DESIGN

Location:	**Santa Fe, New Mexico**
Type of system:	Active rooftop
Year installed:	2006
Annual rainfall:	Average 14 inches
Catchment area:	Rooftop — Approx. 30,953 square feet for ten casita units
Containment:	Below-grade Darco tank system, nine 18,000-gallon and eight 16,000-gallon.
Annual quantity collected:	250,053 gallons
Water usage:	Landscape irrigation
Equipment involved:	Pumps — Grundfos SQE submersible pump Cistern level controls — Digital water quality indicating system Pressure tank — Not available Filters — Inline convenience filter, Graf Universal large scale filter system
Contact:	A Desert Rain System by The Hydro Group, Santa Fe, New Mexico www.thehydrosgroup.com

for horseback riding, and hiking opportunities. Horses can also be boarded at the 92-stall equestrian center on the property.

Each home in the community has a rainwater catchment system. At the Casitas, ten units have been linked into two clusters of Darco tanks providing 18,000 gallons of water storage in one cluster and 16,000 gallons in the other. The system will supply water to the irrigation system through the DRS switching system. The pump system used is a Grundfos SQE Submersible System. The filter system is the Graf Universal large scale filter system that filters 100 percent of the water conveyed to the cistern system. The system also has an automatic dial feature that will notify The Hydros Group if anything should malfunction.

Commercial Rainwater Harvesting Systems

CABELL BRAND STORE—RECREATIONAL FACILITY

Cabell Brand's system is located in Salem, Virginia. The building was constructed in the 1960s and is used as a recreational facility. The building houses a full tennis court, a basketball court, showers, weight room, and is adjacent to a swimming pool. The gutter system was redesigned to carry all the roof water inside the building to the roof washers.

Mr. Brand was experiencing $600 per month water bills from

The two cisterns located at the back of the building, with the three roof washers above the tanks

ED CRAWFORD, RAINWATER MANAGEMENT SOLUTIONS

Location:	Salem, Virginia
Type of system:	Active rooftop
Year installed:	2003
Annual rainfall:	42 inches
Catchment area:	Rooftop — 10,000 square feet, metal building constructed in late 1960s
Containment:	Two 10,000-gallon above ground, black, UV-protected tanks
Annual quantity collected:	252,000 gallons
Water usage:	Landscape irrigation and pool replenishment (potable system)
Equipment involved:	Pumps — Jet pump Cistern level controls — Float switches Pressure tank — Not available Filters — Three roof washers, floating cistern filter in one tank, in-line sediment filter, in-line carbon filter, and a UV light
Contact:	Rainwater Management Solutions, Salem, Virginia www.rainwatermanagement.com

the municipal water supply to operate the gym and pool. The pool is open year round. The goal was to reduce the water cost by 70 percent. After installing the system the water bill has been reduced by 65-75 percent. The remaining cost for water is mostly due to use in the building.

All of the rainwater from the building is filtered and stored in the 10,000 gallon tanks. Any overflow from the tanks is used to recharge the ground water through gravel and black fill pipe.

Mr. Brand has used the system as a model to show local, state, and federal elected officials how to manage stormwater by rainwater harvesting, while also reducing his costs for municipal water supply. The end result was the elimination of 6,000 gallons of runoff per 1 inch of rainfall. The estimated cost of the system is $30,000.

EGGLESTON LAUNDRY—NON-PROFIT ORGANIZATION

The Eggleston Services, a non-profit organization in Norfolk, Virginia, is dedicated to providing work opportunities for people with severe disabilities. The rainwater catchment system is integrated into the 34,000 sq. ft. laundry facility in an effort to reduce cost of water, energy, and chemicals. The rainwater is channeled from the all-rubber roof into a network of drain-pipes in the ceiling to the two 10,000-gallon polyethylene tanks located at the back of the facility. The rainwater is maintained in the storage tanks at an ambient temperature of 82 degrees, thus reducing the energy required to heat the washing water.

The rainwater is pumped out of the tanks with a floating cistern filter and through three separate filtration systems into the laundry building where it is used as washing water. The water is used for washing machines instead of using

ED CRAWFORD, RAINWATER MANAGEMENT SOLUTIONS

ED CRAWFORD, RAINWATER MANAGEMENT SOLUTIONS

*Front of the
Eggleston Services
building*

*Two rainwater
tanks*

Location:	**Norfolk, Virginia**
Type of system:	Active rooftop
Year installed:	2002
Annual rainfall:	Approx. 40 inches
Catchment area:	Rooftop — 34,000 square feet
Containment:	Two above-grade 10,000-gallon polyethylene tanks
Annual quantity collected:	897,600 gallons
Water usage:	Washing machine water
Equipment involved:	Pumps — Jet pump, automatic switch to municipal water if cistern is dry Cistern level controls — Float switches and level sensor Pressure tank — Yes Filters — Floating cistern filter in one tank, bag filter, in-line sediment filter, in-line carbon filter, and a UV light
Contact:	Rainwater Management Solutions, Salem, Virginia www.rainwatermanagement.com

municipal water from the City of Norfolk. The company conducts services for 4.5 million pounds of laundry per year. By using rainwater, the center has experienced multiple savings in reduced soap and softeners because the rainwater is already soft and in energy saving as less heat is required in the washing process because of the stored temperature of the rainwater.

To help with the water heating, the company added a 30-foot-long heat exchanger system; the heat from the wash tunnel waste water will now be used to warm the domestic water or rainwater entering the building. The rainwater system is an automated system switching from rainwater to municipal water when rainwater is not available. Rainwater is additionally fed into the boilers to partially fuel the steam-heated ironers. The harvested rainwater provides up to 15 percent of the laundry's water requirements. Based on the average rainfall, the system yields seventy-two days of laundry operation. The approximate cost of the system was $30,000 and the return on the rainwater harvesting system was 12 months.

EL MONTE SAGRADO—LIVING RESORT AND SPA

The El Monte Sagrado Living Resort and Spa is a 4-acre luxury resort nestled into the Taos historic urban downtown. The site takes its architectural craftsmanship details from the area's Native American roots and incorporates local building materials, as well as using green building techniques to create innovative, cutting-

Location:	Taos, New Mexico
Type of system:	Active rooftop and stormwater system
Year installed:	2003
Annual rainfall:	12 inches rain and 35 inches snow
Catchment area:	Four acres Rooftop — 70,189 square feet Ground level — 210,000 square feet
Containment:	Below-grade; two 13,000-gallon tanks for a total water storage of 26,000 gallons
Annual quantity collected:	Approx. 1.9 million gallons
Water usage:	Landscape irrigation
Equipment involved:	Pumps — Lift station pumps, pond circulation pumps, and rainwater pumps (Grundfos) Cistern level controls — Multiple float switches Pressure tank — 200 gallon Filters — Sediment and micron
Contact:	Developer — Thomas Worrell Jr., Living Designs Group Architect and Rainwater Consultants www.elmontesagrado.com www.livingdesignsgroup.com

TOP:
Trout pond construction
BOTTOM:
Cascade construction

Historic acequia, or irrigation ditch, runs along the perimeter of the site. Runoff from the spa and four adjacent guest suites are channeled to the ditch

Upstream bridge crosses the cascading water

LEFT:
Downstream bridge crosses below a smaller cascade
RIGHT:
Stormwater ponds

Living Machine bioreactor

Douglas Patterson, Living Designs Group

Stream next to building

Douglas Patterson, Living Designs Group

edge technologies. Thirty percent of the complex is exothermally heated and cooled. The remaining portion of the site's facilities relies on energy produced through photovoltaic solar panels. Virtually all wastewater is recycled through a purification system called the Living Machine and is used for landscape irrigation.

Rainwater is collected, filtered, and used in the spa, and stormwater is collected and used to replenish ponds and waterfalls. The complex includes a 30,000 square-foot main building, 36 grouped guest suites, and 12 casitas. The key system components are collection, filtration, subsurface conveyance, lift station, rock sediment prefilter, storage, treatment (Tidal Wetland Living Machine), display ponds, and site irrigation. The rainwater collection and reuse costs were approximately $190,000.

The goal for the eco-resort is to be self-sufficient within five years; the resort is currently LEED Certified.

EARTH RANGERS HEADQUARTERS—ANIMAL REHABILITATION CENTER

The 31-acre Earth Rangers site located in Woodbridge north of Toronto, Canada is a showcase of sustainable design techniques ranging from an 8,800 square-foot permeable parking lot to its 100 percent radiant-heated and cooled concrete floors and ceilings to its rainwater harvesting system. The Earth Rangers Center is capable of entertaining over 100,000 human visitors yearly, as well as capable of treating and rehabilitating 5,000 animals annually. The center is one of the most advanced wildlife hospitals in the world.

Location:	Woodbridge, Canada
Type of system:	Active rooftop
Year installed:	2004
Annual rainfall:	32.2 in.
Catchment area:	Rooftop — 62,350 square feet Ground level — permeable parking lot.
Containment:	Below-grade 84,535-gallon concrete cistern and an 8,000-gallon ZENON tank
Annual quantity collected:	1.1 million gallons
Water usage:	Non-potable uses such as cleaning, washing floors, and pond replenishment
Equipment involved:	Pumps — Not available Cistern level controls — Not available Pressure tank — Not available Filters — ZENON wastewater treatment system
Contact:	Earth Rangers www.earthrangers.ca www.zenon.com

PHIL RUHL, EARTH RANGERS

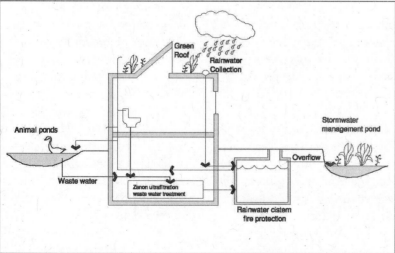

SOURCE: ADAPTED FROM EARTH RANGERS DETAIL

TOP:
The 84,535-gallon below-grade rainwater cistern under construction
BOTTOM:
Conceptual rainwater processing

The water used on site can be classified in several ways. Potable water requirements are supplied from an on-site well. Other water needs are met by combining treated wastewater and captured rainwater. On-site wastewater is treated to tertiary levels using a ZENON membrane bioreactor and UV-light sterilization. The ZENON membrane bioreactor treats the sanitary wastewater on-site; the water is then drawn back into the building where it is mixed with rainwater. The combined water supplies are stored in a 79,252 gallon reservoir from which the water is used for the facility's urinals, toilets, animal ponds, irrigation, and floor/cage washing.

Occasionally the system reaches capacity of its reservoir and overflows into a small swale. The swale, in turn, goes to the Humber River tributary. Water quality of the system must be high to guarantee that these events do not pollute the river environments. Rainwater is also used for fire protection. Rainwater is harvested from the rooftop and stored in a buried 84,535-gallon concrete tank.

GRAND PRAIRIE ANIMAL SHELTER—PRAIRIE PAWS ADOPTION CENTER

Location:	Grand Prairie, Texas
Type of system:	Active rooftop
Year installed:	2003
Annual rainfall:	Approx. 33 inches
Catchment area:	Rooftop – 7,500 square feet
Containment:	Above-grade 15,000-gallon fiberglass
Annual quantity collected:	138,848 gallons
Water usage:	Washing machine water
Equipment involved:	Pumps – Landscape irrigation size Cistern level controls – Equilibrium tube in building Pressure tank – None Filters – Not available
Contact:	Grand Prairie Animal Shelter Schrickel, Rollins and Associates www.gptx.org

The Prairie Paws Adoption Center (PPAC) is a 15,000 square-foot municipal animal shelter for the City of Grand Prairie, Texas and houses the Animal Services Division. Construction began in 2002 and building was completed in October 2003. Total design and construction came in at $3.5 million. Land costs were not an issue because PPAC was built within the boundaries of 171 acres of city land.

The cistern was not a part of the original design for the PPAC, but was part of a mid-construction attempt to make the building and grounds a site for environmental education as well as pet adoptions. Schrickel, Rollins and Associates, Inc. were responsible for the cistern and landscape design, although the idea was the result of a visit by the Environmental Services Director to a McKinney Public Elementary school. McKinney schools are built with conservation in mind and have several environmental- education ideas incorporated into their design. The cistern and equilibrium tube are their ideas.

The courtyard gutters are made from aluminum and collect rainwater from roughly half of the roof surface. The building is U-shaped, with the connecting roof clad in metal for aesthetic reasons. The gutters feed into an aqueduct that connects to the cistern. The cistern was installed above grade and has a copper plate attached to the exterior

Front of the animal
shelter with the entry
rainwater tank

Aqueduct
over entry

Animal shelter courtyard
with aqueduct in back-
ground

Aqueduct
and cistern

LEFT:
Equilibrium tube in the
building, used to show
the depth of water in
the rainwater tank
RIGHT:
Equilibrium
tube sign

Grand Prairie
Animal Shelter
cistern schematic

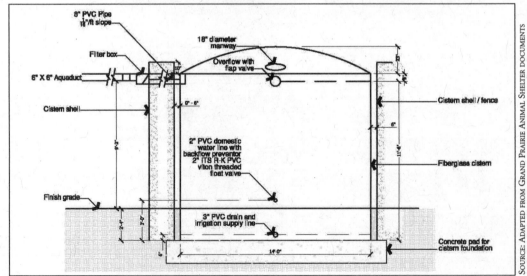

with a quote from Benjamin Franklin, "When the well is dry, we know the worth of water."

The cistern is fiberglass (manufactured by L.F. Manufacturing, Inc.) and is clad in split-face slump block. It is connected to the courtyard sprinkler system through a small pump. The irrigation system has a municipal backup fill for the tank if no rainwater is available. The cistern can hold 15,000 gallons of rainwater, and has an overflow on the west side that flows into a storm drain. Water also backs up and out of the aqueduct when the water flow into the cistern exceeds the capacity of the overflow pipe.

The cistern includes a small PVC pipe, which is buried beneath the courtyard and connects to an equilibrium tube in the lobby. The tube shows the water level in the cistern. Unfortunately, this connection has proven to be the Achilles heel of the whole system as it has broken twice, leading to the draining of the cistern.

LADY BIRD JOHNSON—WILDFLOWER CENTER

The Lady Bird Johnson Wildflower Center located in Austin, Texas makes rainwater collection an important component of the Center's operations. Rainwater collection has been a part of the Center's mission since its establishment in 1982. The Center's rainwater collection system has been incorporated into the facilities, architecture starting with the white rock clad, 6,000-gallon Entry Cistern and aqueduct that escorts visitors into the Center's courtyard. Rooftop rainwater is delivered to the Entry Cistern via

LEFT:
Aqueduct to Entry Cistern
RIGHT:
Entry Cistern

HEATHER KINKADE-LEVARIO

HEATHER KINKADE-LEVARIO

Location:	Austin, Texas
Type of system:	Active rooftop
Year installed:	1982
Annual rainfall:	30 inches
Catchment area:	Rooftop — 18,839 square feet
Containment:	Above- and below-grade, 70,000 gallons in metal and rock tanks
Annual quantity collected:	333,096 gallons
Water usage:	Landscape irrigation
Equipment involved:	Pumps — Lift pump and a high-velocity well pump in the storage tanks Cistern level controls — Manual gate valve and gravity flow to the lift station Pressure tank — Approx. 75 to 100 gallons Filters — Wire mesh debris filter where rainwater enters the cisterns
Contact:	Lady Bird Johnson Wildflower Center www.wildflower.org/?nd=rainwater

the aqueduct. A second cistern—the 10,000-gallon Tower Cistern—is also made from local white rock. However, only the walls of the tower are rock—the cistern itself is located below grade. Rainwater entering the Tower Cistern is delivered to the upper levels of the tower and is allowed to fall to the floor of the tower where a floor grate directs the water into the cistern. A third smaller cistern is located at the Little House.

The Little House Cistern is an independent system, storing rainwater for that area of the Center. The Entry Cistern is an end-of-the-line collection system that is connected to a drip irrigation system that provides water to the visitor parking and drop-off area landscape. The Tower Cistern and

HEATHER KINKADE-LEVARIO

TOP LEFT:
Tower Cistern
TOP RIGHT:
Little House 2,500-gallon cistern
BOTTOM LEFT:
Butterfly roof on one building
BOTTOM RIGHT:
Gutter from metal roof transporting rainwater over walkway to an open-air cistern inlet

HEATHER KINKADE-LEVARIO

HEATHER KINKADE-LEVARIO

LEFT: Funnel collection device

RIGHT: Metal roof on commercial building drops rainwater to a metal canopy over windows and doors, which in turn allows rainwater to collect in steel gutter next to building wall

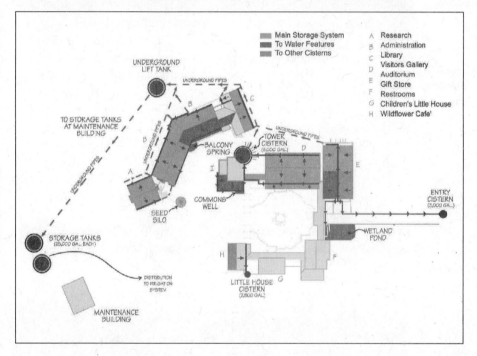

SOURCE: ADAPTED FROM THE LADY BIRD JOHNSON WILDFLOWER CENTER SITE PLAN

Rainwater harvesting system schematic for the Lady Bird Johnson Wildflower Center

the remaining Center's rooftop gutter collection system are directed through underground pipes to an underground lift tank at the northern edge of the building complex.

Pumps lift the collected rainwater into two 25,000-gallon tanks. These two storage tanks are connected to the Center's irrigation system, and are designed to overflow, if needed, to the adjacent landscape. The entire Lady Bird Johnson Wildflower Center rainwater system cost is estimated at $250,000.

Industrial Rainwater Harvesting Systems

FORD MOTOR COMPANY—FORD ROUGE CENTER

Location:	Dearborn, Michigan
Type of system:	Active rooftop and passive 600-acre stormwater system
Year installed:	2000
Annual rainfall:	31.2 inches
Catchment area:	Rooftop – 32,000 square-foot Visitor Center rooftop collection
Containment:	Above-grade 12,500-gallon cistern
Annual quantity collected:	560,102 gallons
Water usage:	Irrigation and toilet flushing at the Visitor Center and filtering of stormwater through porous pavement
Equipment involved:	Pumps – Two at the Visitor Center Cistern level controls – Two-stage level switch Meroid Series 500 float switch; digital control panel with low-volume alarm Pressure tank – 80 gallons and two booster pumps Filters – Ten-inch roof drain passes through a 10-inch strainer prior to entering tank, 10-micron final filter with automatic switchover
Contact:	Ford Motor Company, Environmental Quality Office and ARCADIS www.ford.com www.arcadis-us.com

In 1917 Henry Ford purchased 1,100 acres of Dearborn, Michigan marshland along the banks of the Rouge River, land that was considered unsuitable for farming. Ford quickly transformed the site into a groundbreaking mass production vehicle factory. The factory, simply known as "the Rouge," was famous for providing a brighter, safer, and more efficient factory than other factories of the day. In 2000, the Ford Motor Company began revitalization of the Rouge Factory. The project—600 acres (the remaining acreage was sold)—was classified as the largest Brownfield redevelopment in American History.

Among many aspects that were upgraded for the redevelopment site was the management of stormwater leaving the site. Today, a green roof—atop the new truck assembly plant—and a large porous-pavement parking lot help cleanse the stormwater before it leaves the site to join the adjacent Rouge River. This natural treatment system saved—at one-third the cost—millions of dollars by eliminating the need to build and operate a traditional stormwater treatment plant.[41]

The green roof, a 10.4-acre Xero Flor™ system, consists of sedum plantings of "Fulda Glow" and "Diffusum," and 1 inch of growing medium, with a 2-inch fleece and drainage layer. It has a total saturated weight of 10 lbs/sq. ft.

The 19-acre porous parking lot was, when it was built, the

Aerial of facility, Visitor Center on far left of photograph

FORD MOTOR COMPANY

TOP:
Green roof over assembly building
LEFT:
Rouge Visitor Center rainwater tank, inside the building for display.
BOTTOM LEFT:
Porous parking lot after completion in 2003
BOTTOM RIGHT:
Ford Motor Company Visitor Center rainwater tank schematic

SOURCE: ADAPTED FROM THE FORD VISITOR CENTER PLANS

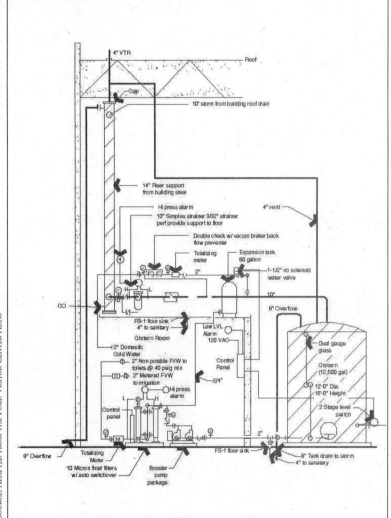

largest porous parking lot in the world.[42] The porous nature of the pavement allows rain and snow to seep into underground rock storage basins, thereby filtering the water before it is directed to the natural treatment wetlands for further filtering. The pavement can store 3.6 million gallons. Four Archimedes-screw pumps move the stormwater when needed. The natural stormwater management system significantly reduces the amount of stormwater leaving the site.

Rooftop rainwater harvesting is conducted at the Visitor Center only. This facility has been certified as a LEED Gold building. At the 32,000 square-foot Visitor Center, rainwater falling on the roof is collected and stored in a 12,500-gallon cistern. The collected water is filtered and used for the Center's surrounding landscape and the facility's toilets.

TOYOTA MOTOR SALES, USA INC.—TOYOTA LOGISTICS SERVICE, PORT OF PORTLAND VEHICLE DISTRIBUTION CENTER

In following with Toyota Motor Sales' Global Earth Charter and "Process Green" initiative, the 86.4-acre Portland Vehicle Distribution Center (VDC) was relocated and expanded while incorporating the USGBC LEED sustainable building considera- tions. Toyota's efforts were awarded with LEED Gold for new construction in 2005 for this new facility. Among the multiple design components selected for installation were a bioswale along the waterfront to filter parking lot runoff water,

Toyota Facility entry

Rainwater 6,000 gallon tank prior to installation

Rainwater tank installation

Location:	Portland, Oregon
Type of system:	Active rooftop and passive stormwater system
Year installed:	2005
Annual rainfall:	36.6 inches
Catchment area:	Rooftop — Half of the main building, approximately 33,500 square feet
Containment:	Below-grade, 6,000-gallon fiberglass cistern
Annual quantity collected:	757,699 gallons
Water usage:	Flushing of ten toilets and three urinals, 120,000 gallons
Equipment involved:	Pumps — Myers WHR sump pump in tank Cistern level controls — Electronic, digital Pressure tank — Proflo by AMTROL, 100 psi, 32 gallon AquaBoost Controller and G&L (Gould) pump Filters — 5-micron bag filter, model PE5G1S by Pentek Filtration (changed every month)
Contact:	Toyota Motor Sales USA, Inc. www.toyota.com

and a rainwater harvesting system that would replace seventy-six percent of the building's potable water supply.

The new rainwater harvesting system supplies nearly 90 percent of the toilet and urinal water used in one year. Additional water is saved by washing only the new vehicles arriving by ship that are equipped with exterior installations—such as graphics and spoilers—instead of washing all vehicles as previously practiced. Approximately 1,000

vehicles are processed daily, or 270,000 annually.

The rainwater is collected from one-half of the main building rooftop—approximately 33,500 square feet—because of the slope of the roof and the location of the cistern. The rainwater drains to the adjacent below-grade fiberglass tank through a 6-inch by 8-inch metal gutter to a 4-inch downspout and polyvinyl chloride (PVC) and copper pipes. Once in the tank a Familian Northwest H_2O FloPro moni-

Left:
Back of house gutter and downspouts
Right:
Mixing tank where municipal water is added if rainwater quantity is insufficient; with pump and pressure tank

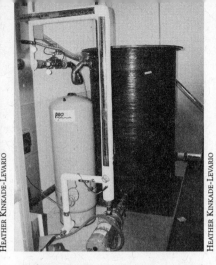

Left:
Municipal water fill
Right:
Rainwater controls

Rainwater processing schematic

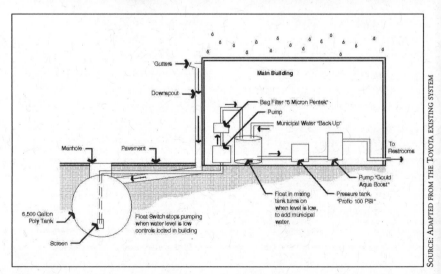

Gutters

Downspout

Main Building

Bag Filter "5 Micron Pentek"

Pump

Municipal Water "Back Up"

Manhole

Pavement

To Restrooms

5,500 Gallon Poly Tank

Float Switch stops pumping when water level is low controls locted in building

Float in mixing tank turns on when level is low, to add municipal water.

Pump "Gould Aqua Boost"

Pressure tank "Proflo 100 PSI"

Screen

toring system controls the Gould (G&L) pump that raises the harvested rainwater to a 200-gallon mixing tank. At this point, if no water is in the cistern, municipal water is turned on to allow the system to operate.

The system generates about six times the amount of water used to flush the toilets. The excess goes into the stormwater drain. Toyota is expanding the main building, and will consider using the excess to flush additional toilets added in the expansion. The estimated costs of the system is approx. $36,800, plus fees and permits.

At ground level, the 86.4-acre natural stormwater treatment is a bioswale adjacent to the Willamette River that filters the stormwater prior to it infiltrating or entering the river flow.

HEATHER KINKADE-LEVARIO

Bag filter and used filter to the side

AMERICAN HONDA NORTHWEST REGIONAL FACILITY

This American Honda Northwest Regional Facility located in Gresham, Oregon is a multi-use facility which includes administrative offices, parts distribution warehouse, automotive technical training, service center, and auto sales. American Honda's work toward environmentally sensitive and fuel efficient products inspired them to apply for the USGBC LEED-NC certification program for which it received a Gold rating. Starting with this rating system, Honda identified every green building requirement in an attempt to use value engineering and life cycle analysis to decided on specific, desired features. Rainwater harvesting for use in the plumbing system, for watering landscaping, and for a natural stormwater remediation process, were among the features selected for the new site.

Rainwater is collected from the eastern half of the warehouse roof approximately 135,000 total square feet in size. The water is gravity fed via downspouts into a 90,000-gallon below-grade concrete storage tank located on the eastern edge of the property. The stored rainwater is pumped out by a submerged transfer pump into the facility water reclamation room where it makes its way through two water filters and an Ultraviolet Light (UV) for sterilization. The rainwater is then stored in two 300-gallon mixing tanks until needed. This stored water is not considered potable by the building system and occupants. As it is needed, the treated water is moved through the plumbing system with the aid of a booster pump and one pressure tank. The rainwater is initially used to flush the facility's 16 toilets and urinals.

A secondary use of the captured rainwater is the landscaping immediately adjacent to the

Location:	Gresham, Oregon
Type of system:	Active rooftop and passive stormwater system
Year installed:	2001
Annual rainfall:	36.6 inches
Catchment area:	Rooftop — 135,000 square-foot warehouse rooftop collection; annual mandatory flushing of fire suppression system is directed to the tank during the dry season
Containment:	Below-grade, 90,000-gallon concrete cistern
Annual quantity collected:	2.8 million gallons
Water usage:	Ten toilets and six urinals plus landscape irrigation
Equipment involved:	Pumps — Submersible Cistern level controls — Electronic level sensor Storage tanks — Two 300-gallon tanks Filters — Aqua Pure Filter (changed quarterly) and a UV Light
Contact:	American Honda Northwest Regional Facility Designed by System Design Consultants, Portland, Oregon

Front of the Honda Facility

Landscape on east end of the building, where the rainwater tank is buried and tank access hatch is located

Interior courtyard irrigated with captured rainwater

Stormwater runoff pond

LEFT:
Mixing tanks
RIGHT:
Pressure tanks

LEFT:
Roof drains
inside building
RIGHT:
Filters

HEATHER KINKADE-LEVARIO

HEATHER KINKADE-LEVARIO

HEATHER KINKADE-LEVARIO

HEATHER KINKADE-LEVARIO

HEATHER KINKADE-LEVARIO

building, which is watered with the rainwater. A drip irrigation system is used to water new plantings until they are established, and at that point the system is turned off. The irrigation system can be turned back on during a drought if needed.

If the underground storage tank runs out of water, a domestic water line which drains into the 300-gallon tanks takes over and supplies water used for flushing the toilets and landscape irrigation. In addition to rainwater, the underground tank is also supplied with approximately 40,000 gallons of water that is pumped through the facility fire suppression system during its annual flow test. American Honda schedules the flow test for late summer, the normal dry time of year. In most other facilities this water is drained into the storm or sewer system.

Any overflow from the underground tank, along with stormwater runoff from elsewhere on the property, is directed to the onsite retention pond for filtration. This small pond has a culvert that leads into a separator tank where impurities are held and removed by a local hazardous materials handling service before they can enter the city storm drain system.

Rainwater processing schematic

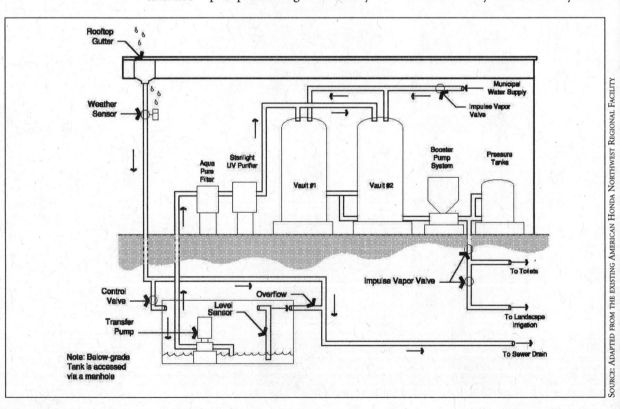

SOURCE: ADAPTED FROM THE EXISTING AMERICAN HONDA NORTHWEST REGIONAL FACILITY

KILAUEA MILITARY CAMP—HAWAI'I VOLCANOES NATIONAL PARK

Similar to the Kitt Peak Observatory discussed later, the Kilauea Military Camp (KMC) has only one water source, rainwater. KMC, located on the big island of Hawaii, occupies about 50 acres of the 300,000-plus acre Hawai'i Volcanoes National Park. It began as an idea of Hilo Board of Trade members for a training ground for the National Guard and a vacation or resort location for the Army. The site has served as a training grounds, a Navy camp, has hosted num-erous dignitaries, and briefly served as a prisoner-of-war camp during World War II. The adjacent Kilauea volcano is one of the most active volcanoes in the world, last erupting in 1983.

The KMC rainwater system basically consists of two divisions—the four raw water tanks (three 450,000-gallon and one 250,000-gallon) and the three finishing water tanks (one 250,000-gallon, one 350,000 gallon, and one 450,000 gallon). In total with the various other tanks the KMC has

Location:	**Big Island of Hawaii**
Type of system:	Active rooftop rainwater catchment
Year installed:	1916
Annual rainfall:	40.7 inches
Catchment area:	Rooftop and catchment fields totaling 6.5 acres
Containment:	Above grade, 19 welded steel tanks with a total capacity of 3 million gallons; tanks range in size from 250,000 to 450,000 gallons
Annual quantity collected:	Approximately 11.5 million gallons
Water usage:	All water needs both potable and non-potable
Equipment involved:	Pumps – Large Cistern level controls – Electronic Pressure tank – Gravity flow to point of use Filters – rapid sand and chlorination after sand filtration
Contact:	Purell Water Specialty Company manages system www.kmc-volcano.com

TOP:
KMC Entry sign
BOTTOM:
Collection surface

TRISHA MACOMBER, UNIVERSITY OF HAWAII

TRISHA MACOMBER, UNIVERSITY OF HAWAII

LEFT:
Catchment surface
collection pipe
RIGHT:
Flume from catch-
ment surface
to storage tank

Sand
filters

Water storage
tanks

19 tanks, used for a total water storage capacity of 3 million gallons. All water needs are satisfied, with the rainwater catchment system totaling 25,000 gallons to 30,000 gallons per day.

They have built additional roof-like catchment fields to increase runoff catchment. In total there is 6.5 acres of roof surface catching rainwater. Once the rainwater is caught it is held in the raw water tanks until it is directed through the rapid sand filtration at 180 gallons per minute. The purification process is completed with a chlorination treatment. Once purified, the rainwater is pumped up to the higher finishing- water tanks and gravity feeds the various buildings on site.

School Rainwater Harvesting Systems

ST. MICHAEL'S PARISH DAY SCHOOL—STUDENT CENTER

The St. Michael Parish Day School Student Center is a multi-use facility. It was built to accommodate assembly uses, performance activities, chapel functions, and physical education activities. The Student Center was designed and built with an integral rainwater catchment system. Each corner of the Center contains a 7,000-gallon cistern. The cisterns are made from corrugated galvanized pipes stood on end coated with smooth concrete to create viable storage. The cisterns are approximately 10 feet in diameter by 14 feet tall. The roof of the Center drains by gravity to these four cisterns, three of which drain to the fourth that contains a deeper bottom

Location:	Tucson, Arizona
Type of system:	Active rooftop
Year installed:	2000
Annual rainfall:	12 inches
Catchment area:	Rooftop – 10,000 square feet
Containment:	Above-grade, four 7,000-gallon galvanized metal tanks
Annual quantity collected:	67,320 gallons
Water usage:	Landscape irrigation
Equipment involved:	Pumps – 1-horsepower Telell 4RJ38 Cistern level controls – Not available Pressure tank – Telell variable 5P22 Filters – Pool type
Contact:	Architect – Vint & Associates Rainwater consultant: Richard Brittain, University of Arizona www.stmichael.net

HEATHER KINKADE-LEVARIO

Entry signage for the school

Heather Kinkade-Levario

Heather Kinkade-Levario

*LEFT:
Outside view
of one tank
RIGHT:
Interior view of the
sump tank— the
deepest, and where the
other three tanks drain*

*View of a second
tank from the covered
walkway leading to
the building*

Heather Kinkade-Levario

*Pump and
other equipment*

Heather Kinkade-Levario

elevation to allow a sump, where the rainwater is ultimately pumped from to supply the landscape irrigation. A pump and equipment room located behind the scoreboard contains the equipment to run the system. The costs of the system, including building and furnishings, were $1.5 million.

HEATHER KINKADE-LEVARIO

Pressure tank

ROY LEE WALKER—ELEMENTARY SCHOOL

The McKinney Independent School District (ISD) was chosen in 1998 by the Texas State Energy Conservation Office to split a $400,000 grant with the Austin ISD. The grant was to be used to build sustainable schools. The McKinney ISD used the grant money to help pay for the design and building of Roy Lee Walker Elementary School and the Austin ISD used the money to assist with the J.J. Pickle Elementary School. Both schools are pioneering the use of sustainable building features such as natural day lighting, rainwater harvesting, and natural and native materials in educational settings.

The Roy Lee Walker Elementary School plan has been used for three additional schools owing to its principles of sustainability and demonstrated dramatic impact on attitudes,

Location:	McKinney, Texas
Type of system:	Active rooftop
Year installed:	2000
Annual rainfall:	33.7 inches
Catchment area:	Rooftop — 69,788 square feet
Containment:	Above-grade, six tanks with a combined storage of 68,000 gallons
Annual quantity collected:	Approx. 1.3 million gallons
Water Usage:	Landscape irrigation
Equipment involved:	Pumps — One 300 gallon-per-minute circulation pump for non-freezing events, plus one well pump Cistern level controls — Mechanical float switch with a high and low level to keep tank from filling too much with domestic water Pressure tank — None Filters — Utilize chlorine and uratic acid for potential algae growth
Contact:	Architect — SHW Group Architects, Texas Rainwater Consultant — Innovative Design, North Carolina www.innovativedesign.net

INNOVATIVE DESIGN, INC.

View of the front of the school, the windmill and two cisterns

Gutter connection through a pipe to the front cistern

View of cistern at the back of the school from the courtyard

View of the courtyard and its sustainable components

Rainwater Catchment

Daylighting

Eco Garden

Sundial

Window into equipment room for kids to see how everything works

Pipes inside the school allow kids to see how the tanks fill and empty as water is used and received during rainstorms

reduced teacher absenteeism, and the students' raised interests in the sciences. The blending of the building's physical environment and the students learning process has greatly paid off, as the building's design contributes to student educational experiences.

One educational component at the school is the rainwater harvesting system. Six cisterns—combined storage of 68,000 gallons strategically placed around the school—capture rain falling on the school roof. Each cistern has an individual filtration system for filtering debris that may collect off the roof. The school has won an award—American Institute of Architects Top Ten list for most Environmentally Responsible Design Projects in

the Nation. The cost of the School facility and furnishings came in at approximately $10.8 million (the same plans have now been used four times, thereby reducing this initial cost).

HERITAGE MIDDLE SCHOOL—WAKE COUNTY SCHOOLS

The Heritage Middle School in Raleigh, North Carolina has been recognized several times for its sustainable and innovative design features. First, the US Environmental Protection Agency recognized the school as an SEDI building, a building designed to earn the Energy Star rating. Then, the school was awarded the "School of Excellence" for 2004 by the state

Location:	**Raleigh, North Carolina**
Type of system:	Active rooftop
Year installed:	2004
Annual rainfall:	34 inches
Catchment area:	Rooftop – rooftop collection 149,925 square feet
Containment:	Five below-grade 25,000-gallon tanks with a combined storage of 125,000 gallons
Annual quantity collected:	2.8 million gallons
Water usage:	Flushing of toilets and irrigation of the football field
Equipment involved:	Pumps – Submersible Myers Ranger 50 gal/min; booster pump is a Bell and Gossett 1531 series rated at 120gal/min Cistern level controls – Not available Pressure tank – Antrol 275 Filters – Watts 50-micron WH SS-B
Contact:	Architect and rainwater consultant – Innovative Design, Inc., North Carolina www.innovativedesign.net

of North Carolina. The school was also named as one of the top 25 Most Improved K-8 Schools in North Carolina. The school system has been promoting sustainable design through the use of Triangle J Council of Government's High Performance Guidelines, a locally modified version of the LEED rating system.

One of the nine sustainable components built into the school facility is a rainwater collection system. Rain that falls on the school's roof is collected in one of the five underground cisterns. The total rainwater storage capacity at the school is 125,000 gallons. Prior to going to the toilets, the water is treated with chlorine to about 1/20 the level required for potable use. A gauge and graphics explaining the system are displayed in the main entrance to enhance student's appreciation of the impact and importance of the system. All toilet fixtures and classroom sink faucets are low-flow and faucets have automatic shutoff. The captured rainwater is also used

to irrigate the school's adjacent football field.

The air-cooled chillers save 700,000 gallons of water annually over the use of a chiller utilizing a cooling tower. Approximately 1,515,000 gallons of water are used indoors per year, 65,000 gallons of potable water used outdoors per year, and no wastewater is reused onsite.

To avoid lawn watering and mowing, over an acre and a half of the site has been modified from grass to more natural and mulched areas, with regionally appropriate plantings. WCPSS required drought-resistant, low-maintenance grass for lawn areas. They will not irrigate the lawns. However, to address the growing problems associated with stormwater runoff and nitrogen that eventually flow to the Neuse River, the school has built approximately one acre of constructed wetlands. The wetlands were also designed to serve as an outdoor learning center. Walkways lead from the school to a boardwalk crossing over the water to an island in the center

Front of school

Back of
school panorama

View with drop-off
area at center

of the wetland and to the water's edge, allowing the students to easily reach the fauna. A pathway on the island allows students to also study wetland soils. These features provide students with the teaching tools to experience and better understand how wetlands are essential to our ecological systems. A photovoltaic panel on the island operates a water aerator, serving as a teaching tool as well as preventing the nesting of mosquitoes.

Combined with the rainwater collection system, the wetland reduces the amount of nitrogen discharged into the adjacent stream to a level of 85 percent below the nitrogen level discharged from the site before the new facility was constructed. The estimated costs of the School facility and furnishings is $16 million.

LANGSTON HIGH SCHOOL CONTINUATION AND LANGSTON-BROWN COMMUNITY CENTER

Langston High School is a redevelopment project for a community in Arlington, Virginia. The 2.46-acre site was originally home to the first African-American elementary school in Arlington. Today, the elementary school has been replaced with a larger facility, the Langston High School, which has been combined with the Langston-Brown Community Center to meet the recreational needs of the County. The project was designed with a "new urbanism" approach, as well as a goal to reach the efficiency rating of silver by the USGBC's LEED program. At completion the building was the first building to achieve LEED status (Silver) in the state of Virginia.

The building has embraced numerous environmental features including stormwater management, energy savings above the ASHRAE standards, maximization of natural daylight, recycled materials,

Location:	Arlington, Virginia
Type of system:	Passive rooftop
Year installed:	2003
Annual rainfall:	Approx. 32.1 inches
Catchment area:	Rooftop — 16,500 square feet Ground level — bio-retention only
Containment:	Above-grade, two 11,000-gallon welded-steel tanks by Columbia TechTank
Annual quantity collected:	279,134 gallons
Water usage:	Landscape irrigation and various other non-potable water uses
Equipment involved:	Pumps — Gravity flow Cistern level controls — Liquid level indicator with float and target board Pressure tank — Not available Filters — Not available
Contact:	Architects — BerryRio Architecture and Interior Design, Springfield, Virginia www.beeryrio.com www.designshare.com

Building front elevation

LEFT:
West or front of building tank that is concealed behind the white panels
RIGHT:
Above-ground rainwater tank at the back of the building

and assistance with reducing construction wastes and increasing reuse on other projects in the County. The stormwater management for the project combines pervious pavement, a bio-retention garden, and rooftop rainwater collection to reduce stormwater flow and improve the site's stormwater runoff quality.

The bio-retention garden collects and filters stormwater runoff from the impervious play/courts area.

The rooftop rainwater is collected from the 16,500 square-foot roof in two 24-foot tall, 9-foot-diameter 11,000-gallon welded-steel tanks that have been incorporated into the facility's structure.

DUANE LEMPKE, SISSON STUDIOS, INC.

DUANE LEMPKE, SISSON STUDIOS, INC.

DUANE LEMPKE, SISSON STUDIOS, INC.

One cistern is completely exposed at the back of the building and one cistern is slightly concealed by panels in the front of the building. Both are meant as "community billboards" for exposing sustainability practices and educating the community. The collected rainwater is used for onsite irrigation, sidewalk washing, and other nonpotable uses. The estimated cost of the system is included in the total building costs of $8.4 million.

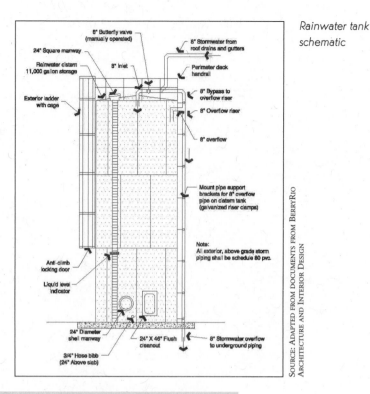

Rainwater tank schematic

SOURCE: ADAPTED FROM DOCUMENTS FROM BERRYRIO ARCHITECTURE AND INTERIOR DESIGN

STEPHEN EPLER RESIDENCE HALL—PORTLAND STATE UNIVERSITY

Stephen Epler Residence Hall is located at the southwestern corner of Portland State University.

More specifically, the building is located at the southeast intersection of SW 12th Avenue and

LEFT:
View of courtyard and runnel that connects in-line stormwater planters
RIGHT:
Liner that will wrap the crates is being unfolded prior to installation

HEATHER KINKADE-LEVARIO

KEVIN O'NEILL, GEOTK, LLC

Location:	Portland, Oregon
Type of system:	Active rooftop
Year installed:	2003
Annual rainfall:	34.9 inches
Catchment area:	Rooftop – 11,760 square-foot rooftop of the residence hall
Containment:	Below-grade 8,600-gallon cistern, Rainstore3 water harvesting structure by Invisible Structures Inc.
Annual quantity collected:	230,000 gallons
Water usage:	Five toilets, one urinal, and landscape irrigation
Equipment involved:	Pumps – Goulds high capacity 4-inch well pump in a flow inducer Cistern level controls – Float switch, SJE Rhombus controls sensor float with mercury tilt-switch overrides the pump when no water is available Pressure tank – Not available Filters – Sanitron UV Light
Contact:	Portland State University Facilities & Planning, Portland, Oregon Invisible Structures, Inc. Mithun, Inc., Seattle, Washington Geotk, LLC, Vancouver, WA www.sustain.pdx.edu www.invisiblestructures.com

SW Montgomery Street in Portland, Oregon. The six-story Epler Hall is a mixed-use building with five upper floors—130 housing units—and one ground-level floor dedicated to offices and classrooms. The building was designed with sustainable components focusing on integrating new technologies to get the greatest benefit from the site's wind, rain, and sun characteristics. One of the design goals was to make stormwater management interesting and engaging for students and residents of the building.

The eastern side of Epler Hall has been designed as a stormwater courtyard with visible rainwater movement and filtration features. Rainwater falling on Epler Hall roof is directed to downspouts that discharge to river rock splash boxes at ground level of the eastern public level

court yard. Water from the splash boxes are directed to flow over and through a 2-foot-wide "runnel" of widely spaced blocks to a stormwater planter. An overflow pipe allows a faster emptying of the splash box to the stormwater planter if more rain falls than the runnels can maintain.

Once the rainwater enters the stormwater planter it must infiltrate through approximately 3 feet of soil and gravel to the bottom of the planter. At the bottom of the planter is a 4-inch perforated pipe wrapped in a filter-fabric sock. The rainwater is filtered and ready to be directed through the perforated pipe to a drain pipe that leads to the adjacent Rainstore3 water harvesting structure. There are four splash pads with runnels and five stormwater planters in the Epler Hall courtyard. The stormwater planters are connect-

LEFT:
Locating the crates on top of the liner during installation
RIGHT:
Wrapping the crates with the liner

KEVIN O'NEILL, GEOTK, LLC

KEVIN O'NEILL, GEOTK, LLC

Kevin O'Neill, Geotk., LLC

Kevin O'Neill, Geotk., LLC

LEFT:
Sealing the liner
RIGHT:
Crates and liner
connection to the
sump

Heather Kinkade-Levario

Downspout to
rock splash pad

Heather Kinkade-Levario

Heather Kinkade-Levario

To conserve water,
this facility uses rainwater
to flush toilets & urinals.
Each year this facility conserves
over 100,000 gallons of water.

LEFT:
Splash pad box, run-
nel, and stormwater
planter
RIGHT:
Sign in bathroom
about rainwater
in toilets

TOP:
UV filter and other building equipment
BOTTOM:
Rainwater systems layout in the narrow courtyard

HEATHER KINKADE-LEVARIO

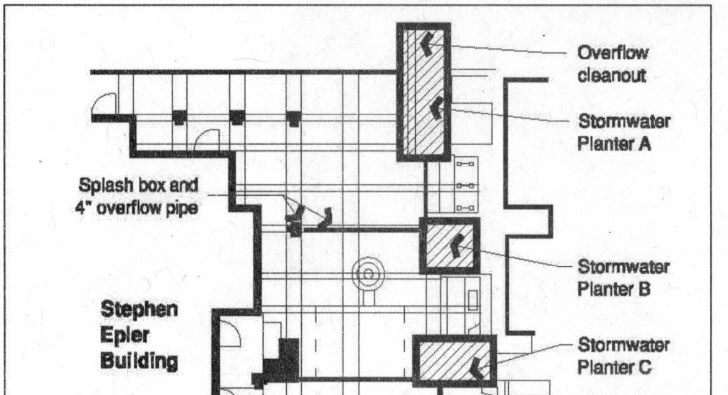

Overflow cleanout
Stormwater Planter A

Splash box and 4" overflow pipe

Stormwater Planter B

Stephen Epler Building

Stormwater Planter C

Adjacent Building

Underground stormwater retention system invisable structures rainstore3

Stormwater Planter D

Splash box 4" overflow pipe outfall

Runnel

Signage

Stormwater Planter E

Walkway

SOURCE: ADAPTED FROM STEPHEN EPLER RESIDENCE HALL DOCUMENTS

accept water to the storage structure if the water rises above the 12-inch freeboard provided in each planter.

The filtered rainwater drains from the storage structure to a sump where a well pump delivers the water to the toilets or irrigation supply line. Prior to usage, the water is first treated by an ultraviolet light filter. An override pressure switch will not allow the well pump to operate if the level is below the 3-foot minimum depth. A 6-foot level of water can be attained before a 6-inch over-flow directs the water to an adjacent storm sewer.

This rainwater collection system and other sustainable elements—such as eliminating air conditioning—reduced the municipal water demand by 700,000 gallons annually. The project has been awarded a USGBC LEED Certified level and a $15,000 Emerging Technology Grant from the City of Portland Office of Sustainability Development's G/Rated Program.

ed to allow overflow from one to the next, or lower, planter through surface runnels. A faster (overflow) pipe is provided to

Parks and Interpretive Centers Rainwater Harvesting Systems

KITT PEAK OBSERVATORY—TOHONO O'ODHAM INDIAN RESERVATION

Kitt Peak National Observatory (KPNO) is located 56 miles southwest of Tucson, Arizona, off State Route 86 on lands leased from the Tohono O'odham Nation. The 200-acre observatory site includes the Kitt Peak summit, which is 6,875 feet above mean sea level. In addition to KPNO, there are nine tenant observatories and one hydrogen alpha mapping center atop Kitt Peak. All observatory facilities at this location (KPNO and tenants) are collectively known as Kitt Peak Observatory, containing the world's largest collection of optical telescopes (a total of 22). KPNO is a division of the National Optical Astronomy Observatories (NOAO), which is operated by the Association of Universities for Research in Astronomy, Inc.,

under cooperative agreement with the National Science Foundation (NSF).

During the initial observatory construction in 1960, the NSF and KPNO worked together to resolve the lack of potable water at the new observatory complex; the result was a rainwater harvesting system consisting of a 6-acre catchment area that utilizes most of the concave road system and the two main parking lots. All rooftops of the complex drain to the adjacent roadways. From the roads and parking lots the rainwater is directed to two concrete catch basins, which act as an initial first-flush device. Combined, the upper and lower basins hold approximately 600,000 gallons. The rainwater is left in the

Location:	Tohono O'odham Indian Reservation, Arizona
Type of system:	Active rooftop collection and ground-level runoff collection, installed due to lack of potable water service
Year installed:	1960
Annual rainfall:	25 inches
Catchment area:	Rooftop and surface – 261,360 square feet (6 acres)
Containment:	Above-grade, two 500,000-gallon tanks
Annual quantity collected:	1.2 million gallons annually
Water usage:	Potable water source for all uses, 3,000 gallons average daily use (no landscape irrigation)
Equipment involved:	Pumps – Large, municipal quality Cistern level controls – Electronic Pressure tank – Yes Filters – See process below
Contact:	Kitt Peak National Observatory www.noao.edu/kpno

Kitt Peak from the highway

*Upper
catch basin*

*Lower
catch basin*

*Backup
supply lake*

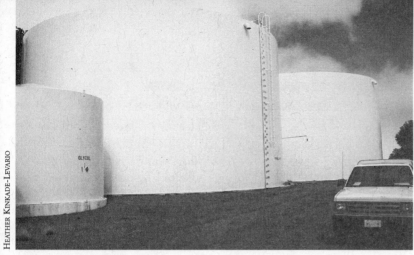

*Two 500,000-gallon
storage tanks*

basins for one to two days while solids settle to the basin bottom. From the basins the rainwater is pumped to a 500-gallon flash mixer and then to a flocculation tank where more solids settle out. The flash mixer adds soda ash and aluminum sulfate to help the settling process. After the second settling process, the rainwater is pumped through a sand filter, then undergoes a chlorination process, and finally is pumped to one of two 500,000-gallon steel tanks for storage. To ensure that there is adequate water for fire suppression, the water supply is never allowed to go below 200,000 gallons. The rainwater is distributed from storage after it is chlorinated a second time and pumped through a charcoal filter.

The complex has a backup water supply, which is a 9-million-gallon (27 acre-foot) lake 4 miles down the road. A 6,000-gallon tanker can haul water from the lake to the main park-ing lot for release into the upper catch basin for treatment when water supplies are low.

The rainwater harvesting system supplies enough water for the yearly needs of all resident and visiting astronomers, daytime staff, tenant observatories and general public/visitors. There are six houses, four dorms, two visitor houses, over 22 telescopes, maintenance facilities, and one visitor center on the mountain. The human population on the mountain consists of 12 to 15 people 24 hours a day, 60 daytime staff, six to eight astronomers, and up to 300 visitors a day, with an average of 50.

Over the last four years the NOAO complex has reduced its yearly water usage by 500 gallons by installing low-water-flow devices. Excessive use of laundry facilities is discouraged, washing of vehicles is prohibited, and all dumping is forbidden to prevent contamination of the rainwater catchment areas.

CARKEEK PARK—ENVIRONMENTAL LEARNING CENTER

Location:	Seattle, Washington
Type of system:	Active rooftop
Year installed:	2002
Annual rainfall:	Approx. 52 inches
Catchment area:	Rooftop – 1,500 square feet
Containment:	Above-grade, 4,800-gallon black poly tank and two 50-gallon rainbarrels
Annual quantity collected:	43,421 gallons
Water Usage:	Two toilets and landscape irrigation
Equipment involved:	Pumps – Exterior in equipment room, approx. 1 horsepower Cistern level controls – Float switch, electronic Pressure tank – Small, approx. 2 gallon Filters – Roof washer, 5- and 10-micron filters
Contact:	Carkeek Park Environmental Learning Center www.seattle.gov/PARKS/park spaces/CarkeekPark/ELC.htm

Carkeek Park Environmental Learning Center was built to provide the existing facility more room for meetings and assembly needs so they could increase their environmental education and stewardship activities. The building has two restrooms with one toilet in each, a small kitchen facility, and a large room for assembly. The building is an example of environmental building techniques including:

- Energy–efficient, highly-insulated building envelope, intelligent lighting, and natural ventilation

- Solar electric (photovoltaic) panels

- Eighty percent recycling or salvaging of demolition and construction materials

Front view of building

HEATHER KINKADE-LEVARIO

HEATHER KINKADE-LEVARIO

HEATHER KINKADE-LEVARIO

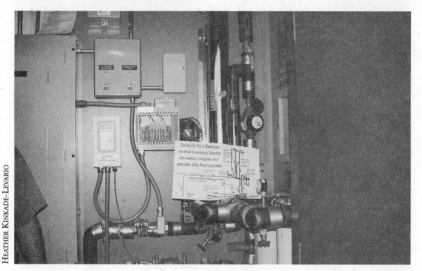

HEATHER KINKADE-LEVARIO

- Salmon-friendly and drought-tolerant native landscape

- Paint and coatings as well as adhesives and sealants, along with wood composite and carpets, are types that protect indoor air quality

- Salvaged and reused materials in the new construction of the building

- Regional materials used to support local economy

- Rooftop rainwater collection for flushing toilets and managing stormwater

The Carkeek Park Environmental Learning Center Rainwater Catchment System is very simple, and is a good example for those wanting to implement a system on personal property. Most of the rain that falls on the roof of the building is directed to the 4,800 gallon tank that is just outside the entry to the building. The rainwater is filtered with a typical roof washer and is then

Pressure tank and used filters

pumped from the tank to serve the building and irrigation needs. The rainwater goes through two filters and a UV light prior to entering the building. The two rainbarrels are used for land-scape irrigation with a gravity system. The Center provides abundant signage for educating the public and has been rewarded for their work with a USGBC LEED Gold Certification.

CHESAPEAKE BAY FOUNDATION'S PHILIP MERRILL ENVIRONMENTAL CENTER

Location:	Annapolis, Maryland
Type of system:	Active rooftop
Year installed:	2000
Annual rainfall:	Approx. 42.2 inches
Catchment area:	Rooftop — 17,000 square feet
Containment:	Above-grade, three old pickle barrel cisterns 7,000 gallons each
Annual quantity collected:	Approx. 402,461 gallons
Water usage:	Nonpotable uses
Equipment involved:	Pumps — Not available Cistern level controls — Not available Pressure tank — Not available Filters — Sand, charcoal, and chlorine
Contact:	Chesapeake Bay Foundation www.cbf.org/merrillcenter

The Chesapeake Bay Foundation's Philip Merrill Environmental Center has been listed as a global environmental model that operates in harmony with the land, natural resources, and the Chesapeake Bay. Their water stewardship is commendable. There are no flushing toilets in the Center, which helps the Center to use 90 percent less water than a typical office building. The Center believes that reducing wastewater use means cutting the amount of wastewater that flows to the local sewage treatment plant. To decrease water further, the center captures rooftop rainwater for use in fire suppression, hand washing, mop sinks, the climate control system, laundry, and washing equipment. Using rainwater allows less groundwater to be withdrawn to feed municipal systems. Less water leaving the site also means the Bay and the adjacent Black Walnut Creek stay cleaner. A bioretention cell filters the parking lot stormwater runoff.

The Center's wood for the sunshades was salvaged from the barrels of an old Eastern Shore pickle plant that was going out of business. The durable wood is a local resource that would have otherwise gone to waste. Three of the barrels were used for the rainwater cisterns. Concrete footing forms were made from reused plywood.

Front of building,
with cisterns *

Close up of the
pickle barrels used
for cisterns

Do-not-drink sign
in bathrooms

The Chesapeake Bay Center's headquarters has won more than 25 significant awards, including the first USGBC LEED Platinum Award in 2001 and the Business Week/Architectural Record Award.

Municipal Rainwater Harvesting Systems

SAN JUAN FIRE STATION NO. 1—RURAL FIRE PROTECTION

Location:	Friday Harbor, Washington
Type of system:	Active rooftop
Year installed:	2005
Annual rainfall:	54.8 inches
Catchment area:	Rooftop — 9,000 square feet
Containment:	Above-grade, 30,000-gallon metal tank and a 240-gallon ball tank
Annual quantity collected:	276,685 gallons
Water usage:	Fire sprinklers and fire fighting in general
Equipment involved:	Pumps — $1/2$-horsepower pump from ball tank to main tank Cistern level controls — Yes Pressure tank — Yes Filters — Yes
Contact:	Design and installation by Tim Pope, Friday Harbor, Washington water@interisland.net

The San Juan Fire Station No.1 is a typical rural fire department except that they have a rainwater collection system on their 9,000 square-foot building. The three-bay station has gutters on all eaves that lead to a 240-gallon ball tank that serves as a manifold for the collection of all roof runoff water. A small 60-gallon-per-minute one-half-horsepower pump moves the rainwater from the ball tank to the main tank. Six-inch downspouts lead to the ball tank, but a 2-inch line transports the collected water back to the tank. The 30,000-gallon metal

Front view of fire station

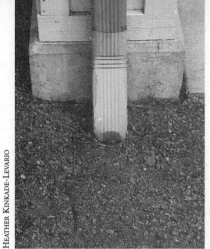

Heather Kinkade-Levario

Heather Kinkade-Levario

LEFT:
*Downspout connected
to a drainpipe leading
to cistern*
RIGHT:
*Ball tank collecting
all downspout drainage
prior to cistern*

Heather Kinkade-Levario

*Roof
detail*

tank sits at the rear of the
property with the operational
equipment in an adjacent
building. This is a simple
system to install and a simple
system to operate, as the water
is used for fire sprinklers and
other fire-fighting needs.

Heather Kinkade-Levario

*View of gutters
from above*

View of gutters and downspout connection

Rainwater cistern

FIRST GREEN POST OFFICE—8TH AVENUE STATION

The US Postal Service has one of the largest construction programs in the nation, owning approx. 35,000 facilities and building 500 to 700 new facilities each year. The Postal Service recognizes they need to be stewards in their building process. In 1993, the Postmaster General issued the *USPS Environmental Policy and Guiding Principles*, which can be summarized as follows:

- Meet or exceed all applicable environmental laws

- Incorporate environmental consideration into the business planning process

- Foster the sustainable use of natural resources by promoting pollution prevention, reducing waste, recycling, and reusing materials

- Expect every employee to take ownership and responsibility

for the USPS's environmental objectives

- Work with customers to address mutual environmental concerns

- Measure our progress on protecting the environment

- Encourage suppliers, vendors, and contractors to comply

with similar environmental protection policies

The above list was provided by the 8th Avenue station and is the list of reasons the facility was built to be a "Green" Showcase station. It is meant to test materials and systems for viability relative to the

Location:	Fort Worth, Texas
Type of system:	Active rooftop
Year installed:	1998
Annual rainfall:	Approx. 30 inches
Catchment area:	Rooftop – 25,500 square feet
Containment:	Above-grade, two 10,000-gallon cisterns
Annual quantity collected:	Approx. 468,000 gallons
Water usage:	Landscape irrigation
Equipment involved:	Pumps – None Cistern level controls – None Pressure tank – Three, size not available Filters – None
Contact:	United States Postal Service Facilities Headquarters, Arlington, VA www.usps.gov

Front of the First Green Post Office

The two 10,000-gallon tanks used for rainwater storage

UJWALA TAMASKAR, UNITED STATES POSTAL SERVICE

*Conceptual layout of
rainwater tanks and building*

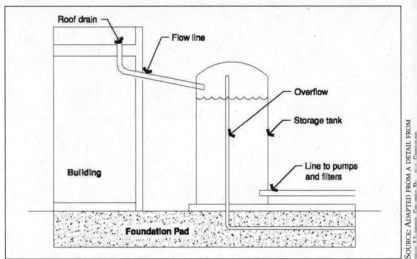

SOURCE: ADAPTED FROM A DETAIL FROM

standard materials and systems typically used.

One of the systems being tested is the rainwater harvesting system. Originally, the system was meant for toilet flushing, but due to water quality questions the system is currently only being used for landscape establishment. After a period of monitoring shows the water quality provided by the system meets City drinking water standards, the system will be used as originally intended to flush toi-lets and put water to other uses that will allow the station to be off the water grid, providing its own water needs. Until the system provides quality water, the water will be used to establish the landscape materials including its native Texas "buffalo grass" lawn. After the landscaping is well established, no further irrigation will be required (during normal rainfall years), and the entire "capture" of rainwater estimated to be approximately 468,000 gallons per year can be devoted to the building and occupants.

The potable water requirements for the building based on a commercial use of 5 to 6 gallons per person per day will be approximately 55,000 to 60,000 gallons per year. The average domestic water use in Arlington is typically higher, at 25 to 40 gallons per person per day. The rainwater harvesting system saves over $2,800 per year in municipally supplied water that does not have to be purchased by the USPS.

SEATTLE CITY HALL—SUSTAINABLE BUILDING PROGRAM

Location:	Seattle, Washington
Type of system:	Active rooftop
Year installed:	2003
Annual rainfall:	37 inches
Catchment area:	Rooftop – Approx. 25,000 square feet
Containment:	Below-grade, 224,400-gallon concrete structure below the basement floor
Annual quantity collected:	Approx. 518,364 gallons
Water Usage:	Toilets and landscape irrigation
Equipment involved:	Pumps – Two large municipal-level pumps deliver the rainwater to the equipment room and a booster pump pushes the water up to the building for use Cistern level controls – Electronic Pressure tank – Pumps pressurize lines Filters – No treatment, only a debris filter
Contact:	City of Seattle Sustainable Building Program www.cityofseattle.net/sustainablebuilding

The Seattle City Hall is part of a three-block area know as the Seattle Civic Center. All buildings are designed to fit together in both form and function. The sustainable aspect guarantees the buildings to be constructed from durable materials and to be flexible to respond to the future. The City Hall was designed to last for 100 years, with the ability to adapt to changing services and technologies. Several sustainable building elements are brought into the designs including designing with LEED, social sustainability, smart mobility, energy and water efficiency, sustainable materials, healthy indoor environments, and salmon-friendly designs. The rainwater collection aspect of the building falls under this last category.

The rainwater system at the Seattle City Hall is located in the basement of the building, where the water storage is below the basement floor in a location that makes it very difficult to comprehend its size simply by viewing the tank through an access hatch. However, viewing the equipment in the lower portion of the basement allows some comprehension of the depth of the tank. The rainwater is pumped from the

*LEFT:
Sign outside the
rainwater equip-
ment room
RIGHT:
Mixing tank where
municipal fill is
added if needed*

PB08
RAINWATER
RECLAMATION
SYSTEM

*Rainwater
tank access*

*Equipment for rain-
water system; note
that the equipment
is below the top of
the tank where the
photo was taken*

cistern to a much smaller mixing tank and then to the building's landscape irrigation and multiple toilets—close to 50 of them. The mixing tank is used to switch to municipal water if the cistern is empty. Using the mixing tank allows the cisterns to reserve maximum storage capacity in anticipation of a storm.

The rainwater catchment is expected to decrease the stormwater runoff by 75 percent and eliminate the use of potable municipal water by 30 percent. The yearly budget for flushing the building's toilets is 750,000 gallons.

KING STREET CENTER—KING COUNTY

King Street Center was developed as a partnership between King County, the building owner CDP King County III, and the building developer Wright Rumstad & Company. The building is located in Seattle's Pioneer Square historic district and houses both King County's Department of Transportation and Department of Natural Resources. The King Street Center has incorporated ornate metal, concrete, glass, and hardscape elements into the building of a facility that has been placed on the County's Innovative Artist-Made Building Ports Registry.

The King Street Center was also designed to incorporate sustainable building design features including resource saving carpet, recycled glass, energy reducing lights, leftover paints, low VOC furnishings, recycled ceramic and concrete tiles, and a rainwater catchment system to reduce municipal water usage. The rainwater collection system was designed by the building's mechanical and plumbing contractor to collect rain that falls on the 44,000 square foot rooftop and store it in three 5,400-gallon tanks. The rainwater tanks and pumps are located on a lower level "B." The rainwater passes through all three tanks before it goes through a strainer and fine mesh 10-micron bag filters.

The first tank in the linear system is a settlement and mixing tank. While usage of rainwater is the system's first priority, a groundwater supply is provided to supplement low water levels. The groundwater is pumped from below the building's foundation. A three-way solenoid valve and float switches in the third tank monitor and maintain the water level in the first tank. The second tank is also a mixing tank where the level of water is controlled by a solenoid valve and float switch in the third tank. If groundwater is unavailable, then as a last resort the float switches turn on the municipal/domestic water

Location:	Seattle, Washington
Type of system:	Active rooftop
Year installed:	1999
Annual rainfall:	37 inches
Catchment area:	Rooftop – 44,000 square feet
Containment:	Basement level, three 5,400-gallon concrete tanks for a combined storage of 16,200 gallons
Annual quantity collected:	1.4 million gallons
Water usage:	Flushing of approximately 118 toilets
Equipment involved:	Pumps – Three booster pumps Cistern level controls – Electronic Pressure tank – One tank is maintained at 115-120 psi Filters – Four 10-Micron fine-mesh bag filters. One strainer and the roof drains to filter debris. The first tank was also designed as a settling tank. Filters are changed monthly.
Contact:	Architect and rainwater consultant – MacDonald-Miller Company, Seattle, Washington www.dnr.metrokc.gov/index.htm

LEFT:
Building entry
RIGHT:
Green roof irrigated
with rainwater

Controls and
pressure tank

LEFT:
Filters
RIGHT:
Three main tanks
in basement

supply that is located in this second tank. A minimum water level of 4 feet is required for the system to work. From the third tank the rainwater goes through a strainer, three booster pumps, and a pressure tank to maintain 115 to 120 psi for the building's non-potable water supply system.

The building was double-plumbed to deliver potable water to all items needing a potable water supply such as sinks, drinking fountains, and dishwashers. The rainwater supply lines provide reclaimed water to the toilets and urinals. The King Street Center "flushing" budget is approximately 2.2 million gallons annually. The County anticipates saving a minimum of 1.4 million gallons of domestic

HEATHER KINKADE-LEVARIO

Restroom sign about rainwater usage

water by using the captured rainwater. This building and its sustainable features is meant to be a demonstration facility for designers, building owners, developers, and contractors.

The building has won the US Environmental Protection Agency 2001 Energy Star Award and the estimated cost of the rainwater system is approximately $320,000.

Rainwater system components for the King Street Center

SOURCE: ADAPTED FROM THE DETAIL CREATED BY THE KING STREET CENTER

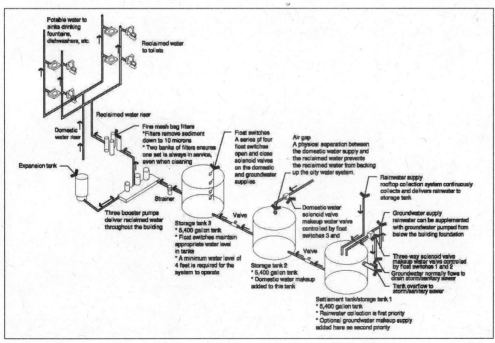

US DEPARTMENT OF AGRICULTURE—RESEARCH FACILITY

Location:	Maricopa County, Arizona
Type of system:	Active and passive rooftop and ground level hard-surface collection
Year installed:	2005
Annual rainfall:	7 inches
Catchment area:	Rooftop – 100,000 square feet
Containment:	One above-grade 3,200-gallon custom stainless steel tank and one 40,000-gallon below-grade corrugated steel metal pipe for a combined storage of 43,200 gallons
Annual quantity collected:	200,000 gallons
Water usage:	Site irrigation
Equipment involved:	Pumps – Yes; size not available Cistern level controls – Yes; type not available Pressure tank – One; size not available Filters – Not available
Contact:	Architect – Dibble & Associates, Phoenix Rainwater consultant – Smith Group, Phoenix www.ars.usda.gov/is/pr/2006/060424.htm www.corestructaz.com

View of stainless steel tank from the ground

The US Department of Agriculture moved their facility from their Phoenix location, on Baseline Road and 47th Street, to just outside the Town of Maricopa, in Maricopa County, Arizona. This southern location sited in wide open fields allowed expansion and the potential for a better facility layout. The new facility allows the dirty field work to transition to the cleaner labs and offices in a linear fashion. This facility contains both a passive rainwater system designed for a visual, educational purpose and an active system designed to collect and store rainwater for site irrigation and conservation of potable water supplies.

The passive educational system starts with the visible and aesthetically interesting roof of the main building, and ends in a very visible way in the facility's courtyard. The main entry building was designed with a gray standing seam roof that drains to the center for a depressed ridge line. The "butterfly" roof drains to the rear of the main building where it drops to a custom made 3,200-gallon above-ground, round, stainless steel tank. The tank contains a floor drain and an overflow drain if the tank fills too quickly. The overflow allows the extra water to enter the

HEATHER KINKADE-LEVARIO

Butterfly roof gutter
and splash panel to
stainless steel tank

LEFT:
Passive rainwater har-
vesting: Channel with
drains to the landscape
RIGHT:
Pressure tank and
equipment box

Overflow from
below-grade tank to
basin for infiltration

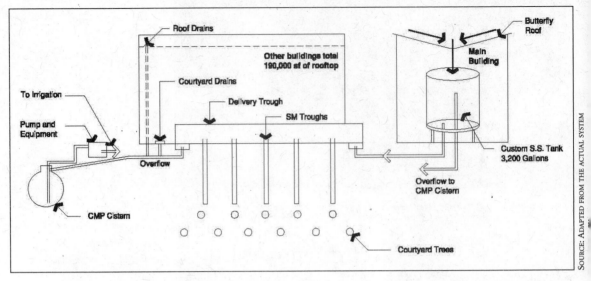

Conceptual diagram of the rainwater system at the US Department of Agriculture facility

active collection system.

The passive system continues as the rainwater drains to an at-grade bubbler box and trough. The trough runs the length of the courtyard to deliver the rainwater to five smaller perpendicular troughs that direct the water to courtyard trees. The courtyard contains an overflow drain and the lower end of the trough contains and overflow drain. Both overflow drains empty to the active collection system storage tank.

The active system collects rainwater runoff from all buildings through a system of roof drains and below-grade storm drain pipes. The pumping equipment and rainwater system controls are contained in a steel cabinet adjacent to a facility parking lot. The corrugated metal pipe (CMP) that is used as a cistern can hold 40,000 gallons. The collected rainwater is used for the 5,000-gallon-per-day landscape drip-irrigation demand.

ROANOKE REGIONAL JAIL—WESTERN VIRGINIA REGIONAL JAIL AUTHORITY

The Roanoke Regional Jail, when completed, will have 605 beds for individuals who have been tried and sentenced, are being held awaiting trial, or have some special problem such as needing to be separated from others. It is a short-time stay facility and will help to solve some overcrowding in other jails. The jail, expected to stand for 50 to 100 years, will be an environmentally sensitive building with energy-saving and eco-friendly components. USGBC LEED Certified level is being sought for the facility.

Rainwater will be collected from the roof of the jail and

Location:	Roanoke County, Virginia
Type of system:	Active rooftop
Year installed:	2006
Annual rainfall:	42 inches
Catchment area:	Rooftop — 290,000 square feet Below-grade, four 30,000-gallon fiberglass tanks
Annual quantity collected:	Approx. 6.8 million gallons
Water Usage:	Kitchen cart washers, laundry, toilets, and landscape irrigation
Equipment anticipated:	Pumps — Jet pump, automatic switch to municipal water if cistern is dry Cistern level controls — Float switches and level sensor Pressure tank — Yes Filters — Floating cistern filter in one tank, bag filter, in-line sediment filter, in-line carbon filter, and a UV light
Contact:	Rainwater Management Solutions, Salem, Virginia www.rainwatermanagement.com

used for washing and toilet flushing. The rainwater will mostly be used for the laundry

services because rainwater is soft water and will reduce the amount of soap the facility will need to purchase. The facility will have less stormwater runoff because the inmates will not have in-person visitors. They will communicate with visitors via videoconferencing from the localities where they were convicted. This means less parking areas are needed, and the parking that is required will not have curbs, to allow a natural runoff into the land-scaped areas for infiltration. Some other sustainable features designed into the facility plans are as follows:

- Vacuum flush toilet units using 0.6 gallons per flush

- Green roofs

- Stormwater catchment and reuse for roof cooling

- Recycling stormwater for use in evaporative cooling tower

Typical jail toilet

- Reuse of cooling tower blow-down water
- Rainwater catchment for laundry use
- Siphonic roof drainage system

The siphonic roof drainage is a technique for sizing drainage piping to allow the drainage system to flow full bore, to utilize the full cross-sectional area of the piping, and to exploit the potential energy available from the roof elevation to the point of discharge. It represents an understanding of fluid dynamics. This system drains the roof runoff to a storage tank more quickly.

NORTH CAROLINA LEGISLATIVE BUILDING—RAINWATER CATCHMENT SYSTEM

The North Carolina Legislative Building rainwater and air conditioning condensate collection and reuse system is working as

Excavation for the rain-water tanks next to the Legislative Building

planned. The system, planned as an educational tool, will help to mitigate the impacts of drought while helping the environment and reducing energy use associated with water treatment and distribution. The system catches 2,292,000 gallons of rain and 669,000 gallons of used water from the building's air conditioning system for a total water catchment of 2,961,000 gallons annually. Three cisterns are located below-grade in the southwest corner of the Legislative Building's lawn to hold the captured water while a gauge is located in the building to allow visitors to view the volume stored in the cisterns.

The rainwater flows off the roof and the condensate flows

Location:	Raleigh, North Carolina
Type of system:	Active rooftop
Year installed:	2006
Annual rainfall:	Approx. 45.2 inches
Catchment area:	Rooftop — Approx. 90,000 square feet
Containment:	Below-grade three 18,000-gallon concrete tanks for 54,000 gallons total
Annual quantity collected:	2.3 million gallons
Water usage:	Landscape irrigation and fountain replenishment
Equipment involved:	Pumps — Ebara submersible, 150 gallons per minute Cistern level controls — RSI simplex pump control Pressure tank — None Filters — Kristal Klear L8830-3FAC-15
Contact:	Innovative Design, Inc., Raleigh, North Carolina www.innovativedesign.net www.ncleg.net/cistern/web/index.html

TOP:
Installed tanks with manholes
BOTTOM:
Tanks being assembled in excavated hole

Exposed manholes and covered tanks

Covered tanks

Conceptual process for the rainwater system at the North Carolina Legislative Building

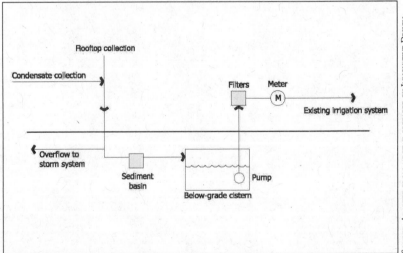

Condensate collection

Rooftop collection

Filters Meter M

Existing irrigation system

Overflow to storm system

Sediment basin

Below-grade cistern

Pump

from the air conditioning units as they come together through a series of roof drains into one 18-inch pipe. The pipe connects to a sediment filter and then releases the water into the tanks. Overflow water is allowed to exit into the municipal storm system. Once in the tanks, the rainwater is filtered, pressurized, and pumped to the irrigation supply line. The captured rainwater and condensate water is used for the following tasks:

- Irrigation of grounds and gardens of the Legislative Building
- Irrigation of isolated gardens throughout state government complex
- Provides water for fountains around the Legislative Building
- Reduces nitrogen pollution into Raleigh's stormwater system

Alternate Source Water Collection Systems

AIR CONDITIONING CONDENSATE—AND COOLING TOWER BLOWDOWN COLLECTION: AN ALTERNATE WATER SUPPLY

Air conditioning has become an assumed benefit of living in an urban environment; we assume the building we work in, have lunch in, exercise in, and watch movies in will be air conditioned. Hardly anyone thinks about it, except for the people responsible for the maintenance of the system. Large-scale air conditioning systems are typically either a cooling tower or a chiller. These units use millions of gallons of water a year to uphold our expectations that our environments will be cool. The water released from these processes is usually warmer than the environment water and can affect the aquatic life by changing stream temperatures. Large quantities of salt and dust can also be released into sewer systems.[43] It is also a large quantity of water that the city wastewater treatment system must accept. One way to eliminate any environmental damage and reduce municipal concerns over the extra water is to capture and reuse the water as an alternate water supply.

BILL HOFFMAN, AUSTIN UTILITY

Rainwater tanks at an Austin, Texas homeless shelter collects rainwater and air conditioning condensate

Orical's Air-conditioning Condensate Recovery System for cooling tower makeup water

Orical's piping to cooling tower

Eddie Wilcut, Conservation Manager with the San Antonio Water System, Texas has put together a guidebook on how to calculate the condensate a system is capable of producing. He believes the rising water and sewer rates have spurred businesses across the country to explore ways to reduce their water use. Mr. Wilcut also believes that reusing condensate produced by air conditioning equipment can be a cost-effective method for companies to achieve their water conservation goals. He has provided the following information from his guidebook for determining the amount of condensate that can be collected from an air-conditioning unit.

From *The Air Conditioning Condensate Guidebook* by Eddie Wilcut:

> The normal, daily operation of air conditioning equipment can produce large amounts of high-quality

water that is ideal for reuse in cooling towers, for landscape irrigation, or for reuse in industrial processes. Yet, more often than not, this potential resource is regarded as wastewater. Most industrial users direct their condensate to the sanitary sewer system or storm drain, where the opportunity to save water and money is lost. *The Air-conditioning Condensate Guidebook* is a resource for those who are interested in exploring the possibility of condensate reuse for current operations or planned facilities.

The Guidebook contains:

- Information relating to heating, ventilation and air conditioning (HVAC) systems and processes that result in condensate production

- Basic atmospheric and psychrometric data and terminology

- Methods and calculations for estimating condensate production associated with HVAC Systems

- Case studies from local businesses that are practicing condensate recovery

- Details on SAWS Conservation Programs that can help large-scale users cover a portion of the cost of condensate recovery projects

Simply put, condensation is the process by which water vapor turns from a gas state into a liquid state. Consider what happens when you set a glass of ice water outside on a warm, sunny day. The temperature of the outside air is higher than the temperature of the surface of the glass. As the water vapor in the air surrounding the glass cools down it changes from a gaseous state to a liquid and the glass appears to sweat. This "sweat" is actually condensate forming on the surface of the glass. The same effect can be seen in the winter when condensate forms on the inside of windows. As air cools, its ability to hold water in the form of vapor decreases. The same principles that cause condensate to form on a glass of ice water or windowpane, and dew to form on the grass, are responsible for the generation of condensate by air conditioning equipment.

To understand the condensate process one must understand the nature of water vapor and psychrometry. Water vapor is ever present in the air that surrounds us. Psychrometry is the study of moisture in the air and of the changes in the moisture holding capacity of the air in relation to temperature change. Simply stated, as air temperature increases, its capacity for holding moisture increases. As air temperature decreases, the capacity to hold moisture also decreases. Relative humidity measures the amount of water that the air holds in relation to the maximum amount of water (Absolute Humidity) it could hold.

At a temperature of 90 degrees Fahrenheit and a relative humidity of 80 percent, air will hold approximately 12.8 grains of moisture per cubic foot of air, but it is capable of holding 20 percent more moisture or 15 grains per cubic foot of air. As the air temperature decreases, the percentage of the humidity in the air increases in relation to the decreasing moisture holding capacity. At 84 degrees Fahrenheit, the same air can only hold 12.8 grains of moisture and becomes saturated at 100 percent relative humidity. At 100 percent relative humidity, the air reaches its dewpoint. It is at this point that condensate begins to form.

While the results of reaching the dewpoint are apparent everyday in our surroundings, nowhere is it more dramatic than in large air conditioning systems where the rapid cooling of air can result in the production of several thousand gallons of condensate water per day.

Air conditioning systems vary in size and configuration. But whether it is a small window unit, a 5-ton system used for a single-family residence, or a 1,000-ton system used at a manufacturing facility, the process of conditioning air is basically the same. Single-family residences and many businesses can be effectively cooled by a unitary system where refrigerant gas is compressed and run through coils to cool the air that passes over the air-conditioning coils. Very large or multi-story facilities may require a different type of system that uses an evaporative cooling tower and chilled water instead of a refrigerant gas. In these systems, cooled water leaves the cooling tower and is run through a chiller. A chiller is a heat exchanger that uses refrigerant to cool and water to transfer heat as part of the air conditioning process. A chiller is comprised of an evaporator, condenser, and a compressor system. The heat load is transferred to the cooling water and then sent back to the cooling tower to be dissipated.

Both general types of systems incorporate some type of air handler. Air handlers generally incorporate an evaporator along with a ventilation fan. As the fan pushes warm, moisture-laden air over the evaporator, the air temperature drops, causing water vapor to condense out and accumulate on the coils. The cool air is sent into our homes and businesses, while the condensate is collected in a drip pan where it is usually drained to the outside of the structure or into the sanitary sewer and simply forgotten. The average residential air conditioning system can produce five gallons of condensate in one hour during times with high relative humidity. When you consider that large commercial and industrial facilities often have air-conditioning systems with several hundred times more capacity than the average residential system, you can start to see the potential for industrial air conditioning systems to produce large amounts of condensate.

Several factors will determine how much condensate can be produced by a facility. However, the predominant factors are weather, industrial processes/human factors, and cooling capacity.

WEATHER

As an example, San Antonio experiences an abundance of warm, sunny weather. In the winter, 50 percent of the days are sunny and in the summer that figure increases to 70 percent. In fact, this area averages over 300 sunny days annually. Maximum daily temperatures during the summer are above 90 degrees over 80 percent of the time. In addition, San Antonio enters a sub-tropical weather pattern in the summer. The relative humidity is highest in the early morning and decreases as temperatures warm up during the day. The average relative humidity in San Antonio ranges around 50 percent in the late afternoon. That's not as much as Houston to the east—Houston's average relative humidity ranges around 63 percent in the afternoon. This is a substantial amount of moisture in the air and it makes a hot day feel even hotter. The result of all of these climatic factors combined is that air conditioning equipment must operate constantly throughout the day in order to meet the requirements of most industrial/commercial facilities.

INDUSTRIAL PROCESSES AND HUMAN FACTORS

Condensate production will also be greatly influenced by the manufacturing processes and human activities that occur within a facility. This is commonly referred to as the Latent Cooling Load. The latent cooling load is the load created by moisture in the air, including from outside air infiltration and that from indoor sources such as occupants, plants, cooking, showering, etc.

Computers, copy machines, and other office necessities as well as lighting and manufacturing equipment all introduce heat into the working environment. Manufacturing processes such as sterilization or food preparation that generate large amounts of steam and heat will increase the potential for condensate production by introducing added moisture in the air. Also, certain working environments like clean rooms require a closely controlled humidity. These situations require A/C equipment to work harder and run longer to maintain specific working environments and therefore can lead to increased condensate production.

Large-scale facilities that are not used for manufacturing can still produce a useable amount of condensate. Human activity alone can dramatically influence the potential for condensate recovery. Facilities that experience a high amount of foot traffic have large amounts of outside air continually brought inside, causing increases in the indoor temperature and humidity. Human respiration and body heat can also increase indoor temperature and humidity. While seemingly insignificant on an individual basis, the heat and moisture generated by a large number of people can significantly affect indoor air characteristics.

Calculating Condensate Production Rates

Estimating condensate production is, at best, a time-consuming process. While several sets of scientific and mathematic equations do exist that, when combined, allow one to approximate the amount of condensate that can be produced at a given time under a given set of parameters, a step-by-step process needs to be assembled. Following is a first attempt at establishing a methodology for calculating the potential for condensate production.

Step 1—Determine the Capacity of your system in Tonnage
The capacity of an air conditioner is measured by the amount of cooling it can achieve when running continuously. The total capacity is the sum of a unit's ability to remove moisture from the air, otherwise referred to as latent capacity; and the unit's ability to reduce temperature, otherwise known as sensible capacity. Each of these capacities is rated in British Thermal Units (Btu) per hour (Btu/h). It takes 12,000 Btu/h to melt one ton of ice in a 24-hour period. A unit's capacity is dependant upon such factors as the outside and inside conditions. As it gets hotter outside (or cooler inside) the capacity to further cool the air decreases as the load on the system increases. The capacity at a standard set of conditions is often referred to as "tons" of cooling.

A ton of air conditioning relates a system's cooling capacity to the cooling effect associated with melting one ton of ice during a 24-hour period. Therefore, a system rated at 5 tons can produce the same amount of cold air as melting five tons of ice during a 24-hour period hour, which consequently would require 60,000 Btu per hour.

Typical residential central air conditioning systems can range between two and five tons of cooling capacity, while large commercial buildings can have systems that range from several hundred to several thousand tons of cooling capacity.

CAPACITY = _____ TONS

Step 2—Determine the Percentage of Total Capacity at which your system is running
Percentage of Total Capacity is the actual percentage of the maximum rated capacity of the system necessary to accomplish a desired temperature. Multiplying the Percentage of Total Capacity by the Maximum Rated Capacity will result in an indication of the actual amount of cooling a system is doing. In effect, a 1,000-ton system operated at a Percentage of Total Capacity equal to 70 percent is equivalent to a 700-ton system operating at 100 percent.

PERCENTAGE OF TOTAL CAPACITY = _____ PERCENT

Step 3—Determine Specific Humidity for air entering the air handler
Specific Humidity (Table 5.1) is a measurement of the grains of moisture per mass of air at a given temperature and barometric pressure. (Look up Specific Humidity at a given Temperature and Relative Humidity). Specific Humidity is expressed as grains of moisture per cubic foot of air.

It is important to note that air handlers will often handle a mixture of outside and inside air. In those cases, it is necessary to identify what percentage of the make-up air is external and what percentage is internal. Inside air is not the same as air directly leaving the air handler. The temperature of inside air will be affected by processes and human factors unique to a specific building.

Once you have determined these percentages, you will need to calculate the Adjusted Temperature. Adjusted Temperature = (Percent of Indoor Make-up Air X Temperature in Degrees F) + (Percent of Outdoor Make-up Air X Temperature in Degrees F). You can look up Outdoor Relative Humidity using real time data on the Internet. You can also determine outdoor relative humidity using a psychrometer.

Once you have determined these percentages, you will need to calculate the adjusted relative humidity. Adjusted Relative Humidity = (Percent of Indoor Make-up Air X Percent Relative Humidity) + (Percent of Outdoor Make-up Air X Percent Relative Humidity).

Step 4—Calculate Specific Humidity for air leaving the Air Handler
Look up Specific Humidity (Table 5.1) at a given Temperature and Relative Humidity. Specific Humidity is expressed as grains of moisture per cubic foot of air. You can determine indoor relative humidity using a psychrometer. Typically, indoor relative humidity is recommended at or below 50 percent.

Step 5 – Calculate the difference in Specific Humidity between the Incoming and Outgoing air
Using data from Step 3 and Step 4 calculate Specific Humidity as follows:

Specific Humidity of Incoming Air – Specific Humidity of Outgoing Air = Grains of Moisture per ft³ of air removed as a result of the cooling process.

Is the difference a positive number?

NO – Condensate is not being produced and you do not need to continue with the calculation.

YES – Condensate is being produced. Proceed to Step 6

Step 6—Calculate Maximum Air Flow
Using data from Step 1 calculate Maximum Air Flow as follows:

One Ton of Cooling = 350 ft³ Per Minute/Ton

System Capacity x 350 ft³ Per Minute/Ton = Air Flow in ft³ Per Minute

_____ Tons X 350 ft³ Per Minute/Ton = Max Air Flow in ft³ Per Minute

Step 7—Calculate actual air flow
Combine data from Step 6 and Step 2 to calculate Actual Air Flow as follows:

Max Air Flow X Percentage of Total Capacity = Actual Air Flow

_____ ft³ Per Minute X _____percent = Actual Air Flow in ft³ Per Minute

Step 8—Calculate total condensate produced as Grains of Moisture produced
Combine data from Step 5 and Step 7 to calculate Total Condensate as follows:

Actual Air Flow in _____ft³ Per Minute X _____Grains of Moisture per ft³ = _____Grains of Moisture Per Minute

Step 9—Convert total Grains of Moisture produced to Gallons per Minute (GPM)
Use data from Step 8 to calculate the following:

Note: 1 lb of water = 7,000 Grains of Moisture

1 gallon of water weighs 8.33 pounds

(_____ Grains of Moisture/Minute) + (7,000 Grains/lb x 8.33 lb/gal) = the following:

(_____ Grains/Minute) X (58,310 Grains /Gallon) = the following:

(_____ Grains/Minute) X (1 Gallon/58,310 Grains) = the following:

_____ Gallons/Minute

The following is an actual calculation of a system's air-conditioning condensate production based on the given data and the above formulas:

System area conditions:

Make-up air source – 100 percent outside air

Outdoor temperature – 90 degrees Fahrenheit

Outdoor relative humidity – 80 percent

Air temperature leaving the air handler – 75 degrees Fahrenheit

Relative humidity leaving the air handler – 50 percent

Standard atmospheric pressure (Sea Level) = 29.92 in Hg (inches of mercury)

AC system tonnage – 100 Tons

Percentage of total capacity = 80 percent

350 cubic feet per minute (CFM) per ton of cooling

Step 1—Determine the Capacity of your system in Tonnage
100 Tons

Step 2—Determine the Percentage of Total Capacity at which your system is running
80 percent

Step 3—Using Table 5.1, look up Specific Humidity for air entering the Air Handler
90 Degrees F at 80 percent RH = 12.02 Grains/ft^3 (Table 5.1)

Step 4—Calculate Specific Humidity for air leaving the Air Handler
75 Degrees at 50 percent RH = 4.8 Grains/ft^3 (Table 5.1)

Step 5—Calculate the difference in Specific Humidity between the Incoming and Outgoing air
SH (Incoming) – SH (Outgoing) = Difference in Specific Humidity

12.02 – 4.8 = 7.22

Difference is a positive number - Continue

Step 6—Calculate Maximum Air Flow
100 Tons X 350 ft^3 Per Minute/Ton = 35,000 ft^3 Per Minute

Step 7—Calculate Actual Air Flow
Max Air Flow X Percentage of Total Capacity = Actual Air Flow
35,000 ft^3 Per Minute X 80 percent = 28,000 ft^3 Per Minute

Step 8—Calculate Total Condensate produced as Grains of Moisture produced
Actual Air Flow Per Minute X Grains of Moisture per ft^3 = Grains of Moisture Per Minute
28,000 ft^3 Per Minute X 7.22 Grains of Moisture per ft^3 = 202,160 Grains of Moisture Per Minute

GRAINS OF MOISTURE PER CUBIC FOOT OF AIR

Temperature – Degrees F	Relative Humidity																			
	5	10	15	20	25	30	35	40	45	50	55	60	65	70	75	80	85	90	95	100
40	0.135	0.269	0.404	0.538	0.673	0.807	0.942	1.076	1.211	1.346	1.480	1.615	1.749	1.884	2.018	2.153	2.287	2.422	2.556	2.691
41	0.139	0.278	0.416	0.555	0.694	0.833	0.972	1.110	1.249	1.388	1.527	1.666	1.804	1.943	2.082	2.221	2.360	2.498	2.637	2.776
42	0.143	0.287	0.430	0.574	0.717	0.860	1.004	1.147	1.290	1.434	1.577	1.721	1.864	2.007	2.151	2.294	2.437	2.581	2.724	2.868
43	0.148	0.297	0.445	0.593	0.741	0.890	1.038	1.186	1.335	1.483	1.631	1.779	1.928	2.076	2.224	2.373	2.521	2.669	2.818	2.966
44	0.154	0.307	0.461	0.614	0.768	0.921	1.075	1.228	1.382	1.535	1.689	1.842	1.996	2.149	2.303	2.456	2.610	2.764	2.917	3.071
45	0.159	0.318	0.477	0.636	0.796	0.955	1.114	1.273	1.432	1.591	1.750	1.909	2.068	2.227	2.387	2.546	2.705	2.864	3.023	3.182
46	0.165	0.330	0.495	0.660	0.825	0.990	1.155	1.320	1.485	1.650	1.815	1.980	2.145	2.310	2.475	2.640	2.805	2.970	3.135	3.300
47	0.171	0.342	0.514	0.685	0.856	1.027	1.199	1.370	1.541	1.712	1.884	2.055	2.226	2.397	2.568	2.740	2.911	3.082	3.253	3.425
48	0.178	0.356	0.533	0.711	0.889	1.067	1.245	1.422	1.600	1.778	1.956	2.133	2.311	2.489	2.667	2.845	3.022	3.200	3.378	3.556
49	0.185	0.369	0.554	0.739	0.923	1.108	1.293	1.477	1.662	1.847	2.031	2.216	2.401	2.586	2.770	2.955	3.140	3.324	3.509	3.694
50	0.192	0.384	0.576	0.768	0.960	1.151	1.343	1.535	1.727	1.919	2.111	2.303	2.495	2.687	2.879	3.070	3.262	3.454	3.646	3.838
51	0.199	0.399	0.598	0.798	0.997	1.197	1.396	1.596	1.795	1.995	2.194	2.393	2.593	2.792	2.992	3.191	3.391	3.590	3.790	3.989
52	0.207	0.415	0.622	0.829	1.037	1.244	1.451	1.659	1.866	2.073	2.281	2.488	2.695	2.903	3.110	3.317	3.525	3.732	3.939	4.147
53	0.216	0.431	0.647	0.862	1.078	1.293	1.509	1.724	1.940	2.155	2.371	2.586	2.802	3.018	3.233	3.449	3.664	3.880	4.095	4.311
54	0.224	0.448	0.672	0.896	1.120	1.344	1.569	1.793	2.017	2.241	2.465	2.689	2.913	3.137	3.361	3.585	3.809	4.033	4.258	4.482
55	0.233	0.466	0.699	0.932	1.165	1.398	1.631	1.864	2.097	2.330	2.562	2.795	3.028	3.261	3.494	3.727	3.960	4.193	4.426	4.659
56	0.242	0.484	0.726	0.969	1.211	1.453	1.695	1.937	2.179	2.422	2.664	2.906	3.148	3.390	3.632	3.874	4.117	4.359	4.601	4.843
57	0.252	0.503	0.755	1.007	1.258	1.510	1.762	2.013	2.265	2.517	2.768	3.020	3.272	3.524	3.775	4.027	4.279	4.530	4.782	5.034
58	0.262	0.523	0.785	1.046	1.308	1.569	1.831	2.092	2.354	2.615	2.877	3.138	3.400	3.662	3.923	4.185	4.446	4.708	4.969	5.231
59	0.272	0.543	0.815	1.087	1.359	1.630	1.902	2.174	2.446	2.717	2.989	3.261	3.532	3.804	4.076	4.348	4.619	4.891	5.163	5.435
60	0.282	0.565	0.847	1.129	1.411	1.694	1.976	2.258	2.540	2.823	3.105	3.387	3.669	3.952	4.234	4.516	4.798	5.081	5.363	5.645
61	0.293	0.586	0.879	1.172	1.466	1.759	2.052	2.345	2.638	2.931	3.224	3.517	3.810	4.103	4.397	4.690	4.983	5.276	5.569	5.862
62	0.304	0.609	0.913	1.217	1.521	1.826	2.130	2.434	2.739	3.043	3.347	3.651	3.956	4.260	4.564	4.868	5.173	5.477	5.781	6.086
63	0.316	0.632	0.947	1.263	1.579	1.895	2.211	2.526	2.842	3.158	3.474	3.789	4.105	4.421	4.737	5.053	5.368	5.684	6.000	6.316
64	0.328	0.655	0.983	1.311	1.638	1.966	2.293	2.621	2.949	3.276	3.604	3.932	4.259	4.587	4.914	5.242	5.570	5.897	6.225	6.553
65	0.340	0.680	1.019	1.359	1.699	2.039	2.379	2.718	3.058	3.398	3.738	4.078	4.417	4.757	5.097	5.437	5.777	6.116	6.456	6.796
66	0.352	0.705	1.057	1.409	1.762	2.114	2.466	2.818	3.171	3.523	3.875	4.228	4.580	4.932	5.285	5.637	5.989	6.341	6.694	7.046
67	0.365	0.730	1.095	1.461	1.826	2.191	2.556	2.921	3.286	3.651	4.016	4.382	4.747	5.112	5.477	5.842	6.207	6.572	6.937	7.303
68	0.378	0.757	1.135	1.513	1.891	2.270	2.648	3.026	3.405	3.783	4.161	4.539	4.918	5.296	5.674	6.053	6.431	6.809	7.188	7.566
69	0.392	0.784	1.175	1.567	1.959	2.351	2.742	3.134	3.526	3.918	4.310	4.701	5.093	5.485	5.877	6.268	6.660	7.052	7.444	7.836
70	0.406	0.811	1.217	1.622	2.028	2.434	2.839	3.245	3.650	4.056	4.462	4.867	5.273	5.678	6.084	6.490	6.895	7.301	7.706	8.112

71	0.420	0.840	1.259	1.679	2.099	2.519	2.938	3.358	3.778	4.198	4.617	5.037	5.457	5.877	6.296	6.716	7.136	7.556	7.975	8.395
72	0.434	0.868	1.303	1.737	2.171	2.605	3.040	3.474	3.908	4.342	4.777	5.211	5.645	6.079	6.513	6.948	7.382	7.816	8.250	8.685
73	0.449	0.898	1.347	1.796	2.245	2.694	3.143	3.592	4.041	4.490	4.939	5.388	5.838	6.287	6.736	7.185	7.634	8.083	8.532	8.981
74	0.464	0.928	1.393	1.857	2.321	2.785	3.249	3.713	4.178	4.642	5.106	5.570	6.034	6.499	6.963	7.427	7.891	8.355	8.819	9.284
75	0.480	0.959	1.439	1.919	2.398	2.878	3.358	3.837	4.317	4.797	5.276	5.756	6.235	6.715	7.195	7.674	8.154	8.634	9.113	9.593
76	0.495	0.991	1.486	1.982	2.477	2.973	3.468	3.964	4.459	4.955	5.450	5.945	6.441	6.936	7.432	7.927	8.423	8.918	9.414	9.909
77	0.512	1.023	1.535	2.046	2.558	3.069	3.581	4.093	4.604	5.116	5.627	6.139	6.651	7.162	7.674	8.185	8.697	9.208	9.720	10.232
78	0.528	1.056	1.584	2.112	2.640	3.168	3.696	4.224	4.752	5.280	5.808	6.336	6.865	7.393	7.921	8.449	8.977	9.505	10.033	10.561
79	0.545	1.090	1.634	2.179	2.724	3.269	3.814	4.359	4.903	5.448	5.993	6.538	7.083	7.628	8.172	8.717	9.262	9.807	10.352	10.897
80	0.562	1.124	1.686	2.248	2.810	3.372	3.934	4.496	5.058	5.620	6.181	6.743	7.305	7.867	8.429	8.991	9.553	10.115	10.677	11.239
81	0.579	1.159	1.738	2.318	2.897	3.476	4.056	4.635	5.215	5.794	6.373	6.953	7.532	8.112	8.691	9.270	9.850	10.429	11.009	11.588
82	0.597	1.194	1.792	2.389	2.986	3.583	4.180	4.777	5.375	5.972	6.569	7.166	7.763	8.361	8.958	9.555	10.152	10.749	11.346	11.944
83	0.615	1.231	1.846	2.461	3.076	3.692	4.307	4.922	5.538	6.153	6.768	7.383	7.999	8.614	9.229	9.845	10.460	11.075	11.691	12.306
84	0.634	1.267	1.901	2.535	3.169	3.802	4.436	5.070	5.704	6.337	6.971	7.605	8.238	8.872	9.506	10.140	10.773	11.407	12.041	12.675
85	0.653	1.305	1.958	2.610	3.263	3.915	4.568	5.220	5.873	6.525	7.178	7.830	8.483	9.135	9.788	10.440	11.093	11.745	12.398	13.050
86	0.672	1.343	2.015	2.686	3.358	4.030	4.701	5.373	6.044	6.716	7.388	8.059	8.731	9.402	10.074	10.746	11.417	12.089	12.760	13.432
87	0.691	1.382	2.073	2.764	3.455	4.146	4.837	5.528	6.219	6.910	7.601	8.292	8.983	9.674	10.365	11.056	11.748	12.439	13.130	13.821
88	0.711	1.422	2.132	2.843	3.554	4.265	4.976	5.686	6.397	7.108	7.819	8.529	9.240	9.951	10.662	11.373	12.083	12.794	13.505	14.216
89	0.731	1.462	2.193	2.924	3.654	4.385	5.116	5.847	6.578	7.309	8.040	8.771	9.501	10.232	10.963	11.694	12.425	13.156	13.887	14.618
90	0.751	1.503	2.254	3.005	3.757	4.508	5.259	6.010	6.762	7.513	8.264	9.016	9.767	10.518	11.270	12.021	12.772	13.523	14.275	15.026
91	0.772	1.544	2.316	3.088	3.860	4.632	5.404	6.176	6.948	7.721	8.493	9.265	10.037	10.809	11.581	12.353	13.125	13.897	14.669	15.441
92	0.793	1.586	2.379	3.173	3.966	4.759	5.552	6.345	7.138	7.931	8.724	9.518	10.311	11.104	11.897	12.690	13.483	14.276	15.069	15.863
93	0.815	1.629	2.444	3.258	4.073	4.887	5.702	6.516	7.331	8.145	8.960	9.774	10.589	11.404	12.218	13.033	13.847	14.662	15.476	16.291
94	0.836	1.673	2.509	3.345	4.181	5.018	5.854	6.690	7.527	8.363	9.199	10.035	10.872	11.708	12.544	13.380	14.217	15.053	15.889	16.726
95	0.858	1.717	2.575	3.433	4.292	5.150	6.008	6.867	7.725	8.584	9.442	10.300	11.159	12.017	12.875	13.734	14.592	15.450	16.309	17.167
96	0.881	1.762	2.642	3.523	4.404	5.285	6.165	7.046	7.927	8.808	9.688	10.569	11.450	12.331	13.211	14.092	14.973	15.854	16.734	17.615
97	0.903	1.807	2.710	3.614	4.517	5.421	6.324	7.228	8.131	9.035	9.938	10.842	11.745	12.649	13.552	14.456	15.359	16.263	17.166	18.070
98	0.927	1.853	2.780	3.706	4.633	5.559	6.486	7.412	8.339	9.265	10.192	11.118	12.045	12.972	13.898	14.825	15.751	16.678	17.604	18.531
99	0.950	1.900	2.850	3.800	4.750	5.700	6.650	7.599	8.549	9.499	10.449	11.399	12.349	13.299	14.249	15.199	16.149	17.099	18.049	18.999
100	0.974	1.947	2.921	3.895	4.868	5.842	6.816	7.789	8.763	9.737	10.710	11.684	12.657	13.631	14.605	15.578	16.552	17.526	18.499	19.473

Temperature – Degrees F

Step 9—Convert Total Grains of Moisture produced to Gallons per Minute (GPM)
202,160 Grains/Minute X (1 Gallon/58,310 Grains) = 3.46 Gallons Per Minute (GPM)

Condensate is generally a high quality source of water, making it ideal for numerous applications. Because of the removal of minerals during the evaporation process, condensate is similar in water quality to distilled water. In condensate, suspended solids, turbidity, and salinity are low and the pH is neutral to slightly acidic.

It is important to keep air-conditioning equipment as clean as possible in order to ensure that condensate stays uncontaminated. In particular, the evaporator coils and drip trays should be kept free of dust, dirt and other debris. As condensate is formed, it is generally pure until it comes into direct contact with such surfaces as the evaporator coils, condensate pans, and drain lines. It is from these surfaces that condensate will come into contact with dust, debris, bacteria, etc.

Condensate drain pans are characteristically located in areas with very little light and offer a moist and warm breeding ground for bacteria and the production of bacterial slime. This slime can ultimately cause blockages to occur in the condensate drain lines, resulting in water damage

to homes and buildings.

In residential settings, it is important to change the air conditioning filters regularly. This will help to keep the evaporator coils clean and help reduce the potential for bacterial growth.

It is also important to keep your condensate drain line clean. To clean the condensate drain line, you will first need to turn off your air conditioner and disconnect the drain line from the condensate drain pan. You can clean out the hose by pouring a vinegar-water or bleach-water solution down the hose and letting it drain normally. This will help to kill fungus growing inside the hose and reduce the risk of blockages. While you may be able to do this yourself, it is highly recommended that you use the services of a trained professional.

In commercial and industrial settings, accessing the condensate drain pans is often easier. In these settings, it is recommended that the pans be kept free of dirt and debris by regular cleaning and the addition of biocide tablets to the condensate within the drain pans.

One concern that deserves special attention when dealing with condensate is the possible presence of microbial pathogens. Condensate is generally created in the presence of moisture and warmth. Condensate drain pans are often prime breeding grounds for bacteria. If condensate is allowed to stagnate and become warm in a cooling system, it can lead to favorable growth conditions for bacteria, including *legionella pnuemophila* bacteria that are the cause of Legionnaires' disease. Although *legionella pnuemophila* is commonly found in a variety of natural and man-made aquatic environments, it can become a public health threat if water containing the bacteria is atomized and inhaled. Atomization will occurs when a liquid is sprayed under pressure, creating a mist. This can occur under such applications as landscape irrigation.

As the saying goes, "It is better to be safe than sorry." If you are going to collect and reuse condensate for any purpose, it is always a good idea to ensure some type of treatment that will help to reduce the risk of microbial growth. This can often be easily done by the addition of a small amount of chlorine. It is highly recommended that you use the services of a trained professional when it comes to water treatment.

Following are a few case studies that shown how air-conditioning condensate is being safely collected and reused. These examples also use very little chemical filtration in their individual systems. Mixing of rainwater and air conditioning condensate with cooling tower blowdown water may also be one way to dilute the cooling tower chemical build-up.

CASE STUDY: T.C. WILLIAMS HIGH SCHOOL—RAINWATER, AIR CONDITIONING CONDENSATE, AND COOLING TOWER BLOWDOWN WATER

Moseley Architects designed a 461,000 square-foot, three-story building with a 450,000-gallon cistern for the T.C. Williams High School in northern Virginia. The cistern is located under the school's parking lot and collects rainwater,

Location:	Alexandria, Virginia
Type of system:	Active multiple water collection
Year installed:	2004
Containment:	Below-grade, 450,000-gallon concrete cistern under parking lot
Water usage:	Toilets, landscape irrigation, roof garden, and cooling tower make-up water
Contact:	Moseley Architects, Richmond, Virginia www.moseleyarchitects.com Hensel Phelps Construction Company Alexandria City Public Schools www.acps.k12.va.us

TOP LEFT:
Cistern floor during construction
TOP RIGHT:
Cistern walls going up

View of interior cistern ceiling and floor at completion

Covered above view of the cistern location

SOURCE: ADAPTED FROM A DETAIL PROVIDED BY MCCALL-TROMETER ARCHITECTS,
HENSEL PHELPS CONSTRUCTION, AND CITY OF ALEXANDRIA

Air conditioning units — Cooling towers

Roof drains

School

Cooling tower blowdown

Air conditioning condensate

Rainwater

Green roof irrigation

Make-up to cooling tower

Water for flushing

Cistern

Site irrigation

Booster pumps

Buffer tank

Filtration and pretreat

Integrated Water System schematic for the T.C. Williams High School

stormwater, air-conditioning condensate, and cooling tower blowdown water for reuse in the school's toilets, irrigation systems, and cooling tower make-up water requirements. It required close collaboration between all designers and the City of Alexandria.

CASE STUDIES:
ARIZONA DEPARTMENT OF ENVIRONMENTAL QUALITY (ADEQ), ARIZONA DEPARTMENT OF ADMINISTRATION (ADOA), AND MOHAVE COUNTY ADMINISTRATION BUILDING (MCAB) COOLING TOWER BLOWDOWN WATER

The OPUS Corporation has designed and installed three cooling tower blowdown water collection systems. Two systems

ADEQ building

HEATHER KINKADE-LEVARIO

Location:	**Phoenix and Kingman, Arizona**
Type of system:	Active alternate water collection
Year installed:	2004-2005
Containment:	Below-grade, 7,200 gallon fiberglass cistern
Water usage:	Landscape irrigation
Contact:	Opus West Management Corporation, Phoenix, Arizona www.opuscorp.com

TOP:
ADEQ tank connection to equipment
BOTTOM:
ADEQ tank in ground

ADEQ buried tank

ADEQ equipment vault

Cooling tower

Cooling tower water collection pipe

ADOA Building

Mohave County Administration building

BELOW: Integrated Water System Plan for the ADEQ, ADOA, and MCAB

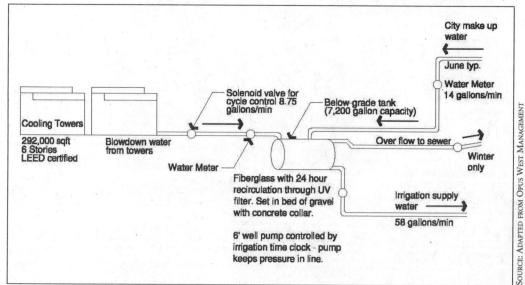

Cooling Towers
292,000 sqft
6 Stories
LEED certified

Blowdown water from towers

Water Meter

Solenoid valve for cycle control 8.75 gallons/min

Below-grade tank (7,200 gallon capacity)

Fiberglass with 24 hour recirculation through UV filter. Set in bed of gravel with concrete collar.

6' well pump controlled by irrigation time clock - pump keeps pressure in line.

City make up water

June typ.
Water Meter
14 gallons/min

Over flow to sewer

Winter only

Irrigation supply water

58 gallons/min

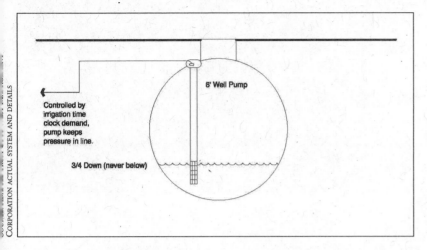

6' Well Pump

Controlled by
irrigation time
clock demand,
pump keeps
pressure in line.

3/4 Down (never below)

Cistern Schematic for the ADEQ, ADOA, and MCAB

are located in Phoenix, Arizona, at the Arizona Department of Environmental Quality (ADEQ) and at the Arizona Department of Administration (ADOA). The third system is located in Kingman, Arizona within the Mohave County Administration Building. All three systems are designed to be similar to the ADEQ building system in Phoenix. Cooling tower blowdown water is collected and reused without any chemical additives for on-site landscape irrigation.

FOG COLLECTION: AN ALTERNATE WATER SUPPLY

There is a small beetle—the Namib Desert beetle—that wakes up every morning, just as the fog rolls in, to spread its wings into the air. The beetle is catching its only drink of the day. The light fog condenses on the beetle's back and rolls down into its mouth.[44] This seemingly simple process is the beetle's only chance for survival in its harsh environment. Humans living in the same or similar environment are not so lucky.

Fog collection attempts biomimicry by placing arrays of fog-collecting screens in the air, similar to the way the beetle extends its wings, to allow fog to condense on the mesh screening and run down the screen to a trough that directs the condensate into the mouth of a water tank, where the water waits to be used. Typically wind and rain are unwanted, but in some areas of the world, they offer the only opportunity for collection of large amounts of water. In areas where the rain is too light to fall from the sky, it must be given the opportunity to form into larger droplets that can fall and be collected. Fog collection takes advantage of this process.

Fog mesh with fog in
the background and
flower in the foreground,
Guatemala

FogQuest

Fog collectors and
tank in Guatemala

FogQuest

Double-mesh fog
collector and trough
below to catch the
condensate

FogQuest

The amount of fog water that can be collected depends on the fog's liquid water content, fog droplet size, wind speed, the efficiency of the mesh used in the fog collector, and the surface area of mesh installed.[45] When collecting water from the atmosphere it is vital to know whether the collected water is to come from fog, rain, or drizzle. The techniques for collecting each droplet size are different. However, fog collection is a very viable water catchment technique in areas where fog forms and water supplies are low or nonexistent. Many communities throughout the world are existing proof that fog collection works; from Guatemala to Nepal, fog collection has enhanced the quality of life for people living in those areas.

CASE STUDY:
NEPAL WATER FROM FOG PROJECT—FOGQUEST COLLECTION SYSTEM

TOP:
Child fetching water from a FogQuest Nepal water tank
BOTTOM:
Typical fog collector schematic

SOURCE: ADAPTED FROM THE FOGQUEST FOG COLLECTION MANUAL

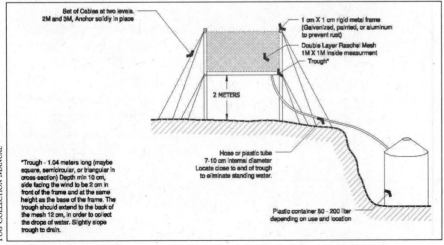

Set of Cables at two levels. 2M and 3M. Anchor solidly in place

1 cm X 1 cm rigid metal frame (Galvenized, painted, or aluminum to prevent rust)

Double Layer Raschel Mesh 1M X 1M inside measurment

Trough*

2 METERS

*Trough - 1.04 meters long (maybe square, semicircular, or triangular in cross-section) Depth min 10 cm, side facing the wind to be 2 cm in front of the frame and at the same height as the base of the frame. The trough should extend to the back of the mesh 12 cm, in order to collect the drops of water. Slightly slope trough to drain.

Hose or plastic tube 7-10 cm internal diameter Locate close to end of trough to eliminate standing water.

Plastic container 50 - 200 liter depending on use and location

Location:	**Danda Bazzar, Nepal**
Type of system:	Passive water collection
Year installed:	1997
Containment:	An array of six large fog collectors (19.7 by 39.3 ft.) to supply fifteen households—over 80 people—with fresh water for several months; water is stored in three separate 265-gallon tanks
Water usage:	Potable water supply (plans are to build a 6,600-gallon tank to allow more homes to benefit)
Contact:	FogQuest: Sustainable Water Solutions, Canada www.fogquest.org

GREYWATER COLLECTION: AN ALTERNATE WATER SUPPLY

Greywater—or graywater—is defined as untreated household wastewater specifically from non-kitchen sinks, showers, baths, and washing machines or laundry tubs. It does not include water from kitchen sinks, dishwashers, or toilets; these sources fall under the heading of black water or sewer water. Greywater is typically only used for landscape irrigation or toilet flushing, and in some states its use and application are regulated to limit human exposure to the water. There are a few rules to follow in dealing with greywater as follows:

- Do not use in vegetable gardens to irrigate root crops or edible parts of food crops that touch the soil; its application to fruit trees has been listed as being safe

- Overflows from storage units should drain to a sanitary sewer or septic system

- Use stored greywater within twenty-four hours to prevent bacteria growth

- Only discharge in areas that have more than five feet of soil to the groundwater table

- Keep systems out of areas prone to flooding (to reduce transport potential of pollutants)

- Laws typically require greywater to be used on the same site where it is generated

- Subsurface irrigation is typically required to minimize exposure; no spray or flood irrigation should be allowed with greywater

- Greywater should not be discharged to a water-course of any type

There are examples of commercial projects using greywater in a safe and efficient manner; it is not limited to a residential alternate water source. Some greywater applications can be implemented through fixtures that exist today, such as the Toto hand- wash cascade toilet. A hand-washing bowl collects a portion of the tank refill for use in flushing the toilet. When fixtures like the cascade toilet are used in the initial design, costs are low. Retrofits always cost more than placing the option in a new design. Greywater storage tanks are the largest cost in a greywater system. A greywater collection system cost can range from a retrofit of $1,250 to a new construction cost of $650. Prices vary greatly and depend on a multitude of factors. In any situation, greywater collection is a viable alternate water source.

Sources:
"Using Gray Water in New Mexico's Residential Landscapes,"

www.nmenv.state.nm.us
Oasis Design web site,
    www.oasisdesign.net
PATH Technologies web site,
    www.nahbrc.org
"Arizona Graywater Guidelines,"
    www.watercasa.org

California Graywater Guide
*Using Graywater in Your
Home Landscape,*
    www.owue.water.ca.gov/docs
    /graywater_guide_book.pdf
"Yarra Valley Water Grey Water
    Reuse Fact Sheet,"
    www.yvw.com.au

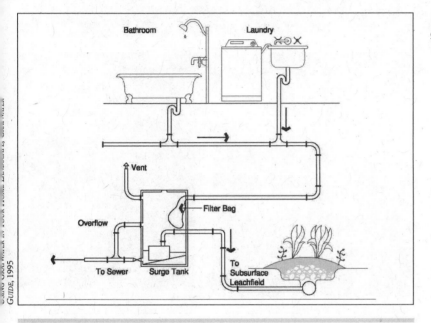

*Typical residential
greywater system*

CASE STUDY:
NATURAL RESOURCES DEFENSE COUNCIL—RAINWATER AND GREYWATER COLLECTION SYSTEM

The Natural Resources Defense Council's (NRDC) Santa Monica office opened in 2003 as a building designed to take advantage of green building techniques. The site was purposely chosen to take advantage of existing services and utilities. The building was redesigned to conserve water and energy as well as showcase environmentally sound materials. The NRDC supports greywater reuse and rainwater collection, both of which are techniques used at the Santa Monica building. The building uses a bamboo-planted cistern to help filter the rainwater which is then mixed with the building's greywater for reuse in the toilets. The greywater/rainwater mixture is also used to irrigate roof level and ground level landscapes.

Location: Santa Monica, California

Type of system:	Greywater collection
Year installed:	2003
Containment:	Greywater system is based on an Equaris Infinity water treatment system, which settles and aerates sink and shower water as well as the rainwater Stormwater system consists of two custom-built cisterns beneath bamboo planters that capture and prefilter stormwater from the roof, 800 gallons per day
Water Usage:	Toilets and landscape irrigation
Contact:	Natural Resources Defense Council www.nrdc.org Environmental Planning and Design LLC www.epd-net.com Equaris Corporation www.equaris.com

TOP:
Front of the Natural Resources Defense Council, Santa Monica Office
MIDDLE:
Greywater filtration tanks
BOTTOM:
Rainwater, greywater, black water, and municipal water conceptual interaction diagram

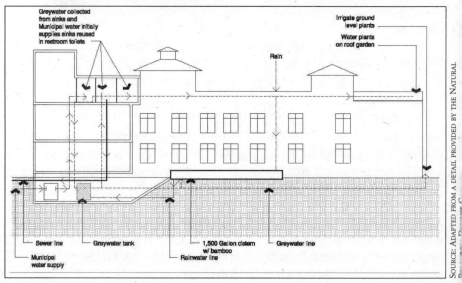

Greywater collected from sinks and Municipal water initially supplies sinks reused in restroom toilets

Irrigate ground level plants

Water plants on roof garden

Rain

Sewer line — Greywater tank — 1,500 Gallon cistern w/ bamboo — Greywater line
Municipal water supply — Rainwater line

Rainwater Harvesting for Wildlife

RAINWATER CATCHMENT FOR WILDLIFE

Remote Areas Water Catchment

Human-made water catchments for wildlife have many names, including guzzlers, drinker boxes, trick tanks, and concrete-apron catchments. Some human-modified and natural catchments are called potholes (human-made rock catch basins), *tinajas* (modified or completely natural rock pools), springs, and wells. Wildlife water catchments are installed to attract wildlife for various reasons. They can be placed to open up lands to grazing, lands that have not been grazed due to a lack of water sources. These catchments can also keep animals from having to tromp through pristine riparian areas, allowing them to heal from over use.

The catchments are typically mobile structures that can be relocated if needed and can help to re-establish wildlife that have previously left because of drought. The catchments can also be removed easily. Human-made rainwater catchments can also be specifically used to attract wildlife for observation purposes, and can be located anywhere in any range or grazing area.

Guzzlers are water catchments that include a solid roof-like structure, a tank, a float switch, a trough, and gravity feed. The roof structure can be built in a butterfly fashion, with a low center and raised edges, or built to have the entire roof plane tilt in one direction. The storage tanks—around 2,250 gallons total—can be built under the roof structure or at an adjacent location and at a lower topographic elevation to allow gravity to move the water to the storage tank. From the tank a pipe runs down hill as needed to a 2-foot-long sump box that contains a flow switch. Attached to this sump is a shallow trough that allows animals to drink; the trough is refilled from the sump box when the water level lowers. Some troughs have sloped edges to allow smaller animals such as birds, turtles, rabbits, squirrels, and lizards to drink safely without the fear of drowning.

Human-made rainwater catchment devices called trick tanks are typically made out of galvanized metal with inverted galvanized metal umbrellas on top. These inverted umbrellas extend out beyond the lip of the tank several feet and slope back to the center of the 1,500- to 2,500-gallon tank so the rainwater drains into the tank directly. A pipe exits the tank at ground level to fill a similar sump and drinking trough as previously described.

Water catchments called drinker boxes are prefabricated devices that when assembled in the field provide the same watering capabilities as guzzlers and trick tanks. However, their water storage capacity is much less. Drinker boxes are usually buried (or partially buried) to allow a low profile and less visual impact than the guzzler or trick tanks.

Concrete-apron rainwater catchments are permanent, and, as all of the described wildlife rainwater catchments described previously, require very little maintenance. All of these wildlife water catchment systems are viable and valuable to the humans building them and the animals requiring them.

Sources:
Harvesting Rainwater for Wildlife, 2006, http://tce bookstore.org

Willborn Bros. Co., www.will bornbros.com

CASE STUDY:
CONCRETE RAINWATER CATCHMENT—RAINWATER CATCHMENT FOR WILDLIFE

The following photographs and details are rainwater collection techniques used for wildlife as discussed above.

They are found throughout the United States in remote locations to help supply water to the local wildlife.

Kaibab Guzzler — umbrella tank

WILLIAM WARNER

Location:	Typical System
Type of system:	Passive stormwater collection off concrete apron
Year installed:	Not available
Containment:	Below-grade storage tank approx 3 feet wide by 16 feet long and inches deep.
Water usage:	Wildlife water source
Contact:	Texas Cooperative Extension http://texasextension.tamu.edu Willborn Bros. Co. www.willbornbros.com

BILLY KNIFFEN

Concrete catchment pad
for collecting water

Raised "roof-like"
catchment surface

BILLY KNIFFEN

Concrete catchment
trough for wildlife
drinking

BILLY KNIFFEN

Tank for guzzler rainwater storage

Drinker box for guzzler water

BOTTOM LEFT: Typical concrete pad for water collection — plan

BOTTOM RIGHT: A cross-section of the typical concrete pad, tank, and trough

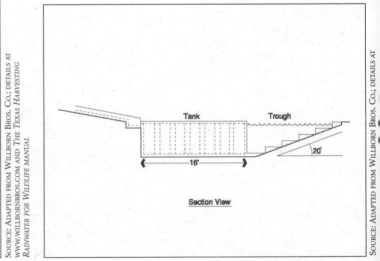

Plan View

- Wing Walls
- 4" Thickness
  30' Radius
  2" Thickness
  4" High from apron
- 16 Covers
  2' Wide
  3' Long
  3' Deep
- Sump
  6" Deep
  (Below apron level)
  18" Square
- 7 Support Post
  8" Square
  4' Tall
- 6" Through space between first step and baffle
- 5 Steps 3' Long
  15" Wide
  6" Thick

Tank

Trough

16'

20'

Section View

SOURCE: ADAPTED FROM WILLBORN BROS. CO.; DETAILS AT WWW.WILLBORNBROS.COM AND *THE TEXAS HARVESTING RAINWATER FOR WILDLIFE MANUAL*

SOURCE: ADAPTED FROM WILLBORN BROS. CO.; DETAILS AT

Calsp

Size: 12 in X 15 in X 24 in drinker box
float assembly coated with black tar
expoxy - includes lock hasp

14 - gauge galvanized steel

Left:
Typical drinker box
Middle:
A typical guzzler roof detail

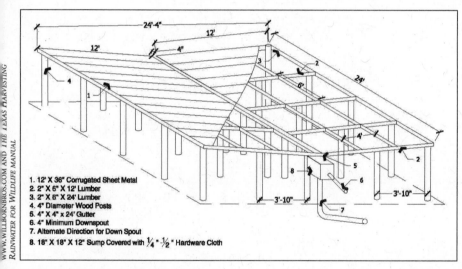

24'-4"
12'
12'
4"
4
1
24"
6'
4'
2
3
5
8
6
7
2
3'-10"
3'-10"

1. 12' X 36" Corrugated Sheet Metal
2. 2" X 6" X 12' Lumber
3. 2" X 6" X 24' Lumber
4. 4" Diameter Wood Posts
5. 4" X 4" x 24' Gutter
6. 4" Minimum Downspout
7. Alternate Direction for Down Spout
8. 18" X 18" X 12" Sump Covered with $\frac{1}{4}$ " - $\frac{1}{2}$ " Hardware Cloth

Float box cross-section

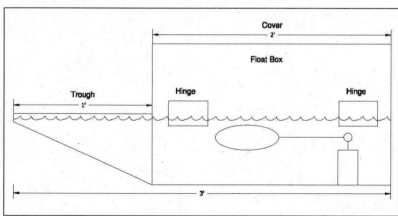

Cover
2'
Float Box
Trough
1'
Hinge
Hinge
3'

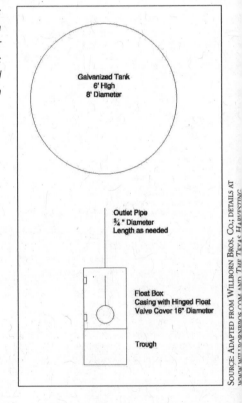

Galvanized sheet metal catchment basin
Variable diameter

Metal grate of heavy wire mesh

Angle iron braces

Storage tank - variable diameter

Guy wires

Pipe to watering trough

TOP:
Typical umbrella
guzzler
RIGHT:
Galvanized tank and
float box plan

Galvanized Tank
6' High
8' Diameter

Outlet Pipe
¾" Diameter
Length as needed

Float Box
Casing with Hinged Float
Valve Cover 16" Diameter

Trough

6 Conclusion

THE PRECEDING chapters have documented and described both the concepts and processes of rainwater catchment, stormwater collection, and alternate water reuse. Common sense tell us there are limits to how much water communities can withdraw from underground aquifers and surface lakes or rivers to meet their current needs without threatening their futures. All of these water catchment, collection, and reuse systems can help offset the quantity of groundwater or surface water withdrawn by replacing municipal potable water as a source for non-potable water demands.

It is evident that we continue, unrestrained, in our use of water. Waiting until tomorrow to save will be too late— we need to begin now. Probably the biggest deterrent to, as well as the main virtue of, a rain-based or alternate water-based system is that it requires owners to pay

It is all about water. When we are unaware of, ignore, or are wasteful in our relationship to the interaction of water with other natural resources, water can become a waste product and potentially a powerful source of destruction.

— Patchett and Wilhelm

German bus wash using only rainwater to wash vehicles

HEATHER KINKADE-LEVARIO

German bus washing and service building. All rooftop rainwater runoff is directed to underground storage tanks

close attention to where their water comes from and how it is used. Rainwater and stormwater catchment systems offer owners the highest possible personal control over a water source and its quality.[46] Alternate water reuse provides a guaranteed water supply that can also be managed and purified as needed. Despite the control afforded by these water systems, the general public seems to prefer paying a municipality to supervise its water supplies. Our apparent willingness to pay for water without question is probably due to the following:

- Lack of knowledge and respect for the true value of water

- Relatively inexpensive water and services compared to household incomes

- Deficient public awareness of resource-sensitive development technologies such as rainwater, stormwater, and alternate water catchment and/or collection

- Limited knowledge of the benefits of these water catchment techniques as an alternate water source

- Concern about costs associated with installing a water catchment system

- Municipal unwillingness to accept alternative flood-control techniques involving rainwater and stormwater catchment

Education of both the public and municipalities is slowly occurring, and the importance and benefits of maintaining the hydrologic cycle has been proven

Typical German WISY system that has become common practice through education and necessity.

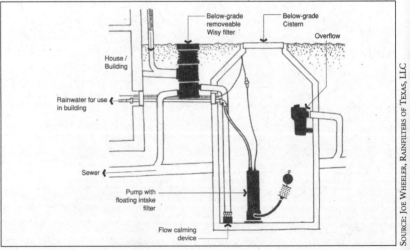

in actual application of techniques—such as the Seattle Public Utilities Natural Drainage System—and in controlled studies. The University of Guelph in Canada has found permeable pavers of interlocking concrete blocks demonstrate a 90 percent reduction in runoff volume and that they significantly reduce surface runoff pollutant loads.[47] Existing projects—as those described in Chapter 5, Case Studies—demonstrate the actual potential for water catchment and reuse from rain storms and building equipment. Several planned projects, and several currently in construction, are designed to use all potential site water for reuse or infiltration.

One example of an in-construction project is the Sidwell Friends Middle School located in Washington D.C., a building designed to earn a USGBC LEED

Rain-catching, shade-providing, upside-down umbrellas in a courtyard of multiple commercial office buildings

Patio and stormwater swale below upside-down umbrellas

Passive stormwater collection: commercial office building with a permeable courtyard

Platinum rating. A constructed wetland will treat building wastewater on site and the treated water will be recycled back to the building and its lavatories. A green roof will hold and filter rainwater as well as grow vegetables and herbs for the schools cafeteria. On a larger scale, the Dorrance H. Hamilton Building and Plaza in Philadelphia, Pennsylvania has changed a formerly 7 percent pervious site into a 40 percent pervious site. The building will collect rooftop rainwater runoff and air conditioning condensate in a 20,000-gallon below-grade cistern. The water will be used to irrigate the landscaped roof of a below-ground vehicular parking structure.

Both of these smaller projects are only the beginning, and the concepts discussed in this book need to be combined with other sustainable techniques to create an ultimate urban design allowing humans to live closer to what natural cycles require for continuation. An example of a fully integrated project is the Portland, Oregon project,

Lloyd Crossing. This project area includes a 35-block, inner-city neighborhood and is planned through a 45-year process. Habitat quality, quantity, and connections will be restored. Rainwater, stormwater, greywater, and black water will be treated and reused. Energy demands are planned to be reduced, and on-site renewable-energy resources will be harnessed. These resources will include biogas, solar, and wind power. Carbon-neutrality is also planned through purchase of carbon credits.

The site has been evaluated from a pre-development water use condition to an existing water use condition to a future-planned water use condition. Groundwater recharge is planned to increase beyond existing quantities, transpiration is planned to increase, and site stormwater runoff is planned to be substantially reduced. Rooftop rainwater is planned to be collected through green roofs and bioswales. The treated black water and captured rainwater are planned for flushing lavatories as well as landscape irrigation and infiltration. All of this information and more can be found on this project by searching the World Wide Web for Lloyd Crossing: Sustainable Urban Design Plan and Catalyst Project.

The Environmental Protection Agency ranks urban runoff and storm-sewer discharges as the second most prevalent source of water quality impairment in our nation's estuaries, and the fourth most prevalent source of impairment of our lakes.[48] Many areas of the world do not even have water supplies let alone fresh water supplies. As a result of disasters like Hurricane Katrina and its devastating effects on the major city of New Orleans, a water-harvesting machine was created to turn air into water. The Aqua Sciences machine can create up to 1,080 gallons of drinkable water from the atmosphere in a day.[49, 50] The machine comes in four sizes. The smallest fits into the back of a pickup truck. The largest fits into a 40-foot tractor-trailer, and includes non-electric generators.[51] The water-harvesting machine works by pushing air through a liquid salt solution of lithium chloride. The compound used in the machine attracts water molecules; it is hygroscopic in nature, which means that it can be used to harvest water in humid as well as arid regions. The water is eventually extracted from the liquid solution and is filtered through

table salt as a natural disinfectant.[52] A final carbon filter is used to add taste. Harvested water from the machine is stored in extremely strong bags with spigots so the water can easily be transported. The bags block sunlight and resist bacteria growth, allowing the water to stay fresh.

A second machine, the WaterPyramid, has recently been designed for less developed countries. It is a hybrid water installation that integrates a large-scale solar distillation and rainwater-harvesting practices. More information on this system, developed in the Netherlands by AquaEst International, can be found at www.aquaestinternational.com/waterpyramid.htm. Both the Water Harvesting Machine and the WaterPyramid are the result of desires to provide potable water for areas that lack clean water sources.

It has been determined by the United Nation's Millennium Ecosystem Assessment that we are "living beyond our means" and that the natural hydrological system is a key service provided by nature that has been weakened by human development.

Passive survivability, covered by *Environmental Building News* in a May 2006 article, is described as "a building's ability to maintain critical life-support conditions if services such as power, heating fuel, or water are lost." This concept has been suggested as a standard design criterion for all homes, apartment buildings, and assembly buildings that may be used in times of emergency. Most of these situations can be remedied with the catchment of or infiltration of rainwater, stormwater, and/or alternate water. It is time to design for water in all projects, at all levels— and just maybe we can learn to live with nature and maintain our water supplies for emergencies as well as for future generations.

Information for Further Research and Contacts for Supplies

Agua Solutions International SA Costa Rica rainwater harvesting consultant, U.S. contact available. www.aguasolutions.com

American Water Works Association (AWWA) The AWWA is an international nonprofit scientific and educational society dedicated to the improvement of drinking water quality. www.awwa.org

American Rainwater Catchment Systems Association (ARCSA) Association for the Advancement of Rainwater Harvesting. www.arcsa-usa.org

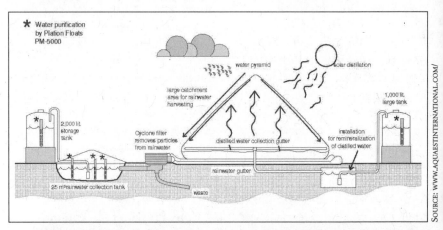

TOP:
WaterPyramid
BOTTOM:
A 700-gallon cistern at Camp Aldersgate Commons Building in Little Rock, Arkansas; a potential emergency assembly building

Appendix A: Resources List

Ao Sara
Offers a variety of rainchains and gives directions for making rainchains. www.aosara.com

Aqua Harvest
Rainwater harvesting design and installation. www.aquaharvestonline.com

AquaEst International
Rainwater purification systems from Zwolle, the Netherlands. www.aquaestinternational.com/home.htm

BRAE - Blue Ridge Atlantic Enterprises
Rainwater technology and equipment company. www.braewater.com/ICMS

Center for Maximum Potential Building Systems
A nonprofit sustainable design and appropriate technologies firm engaged in education, demonstration, and research. www.cmpbs.org

Centre for Science and Environment
An independent, public Indian interest organization, which provides several rainwater related publications such as *A Water Harvesting Manual for Urban Areas*; *Case Studies from Delhi: Drought? Try Capturing the Rain*; and *Dying Wisdom: Rise, Fall, and Potential of India's Traditional Water Harvesting Systems*. www.cseindia.org

Cherry Blossom Gardens
Japanese garden supplies and ornaments, including rainchains.

www.cherryblossomgardens.com

Contech Construction Products Inc.
Offers corrugated metal pipe underground detention/retention for large systems. www.contech-cpi.com

Darco Incorporated
Darco tanks www.darcoinc.com/septic-tanks.html

Demossing Roofs
University of Alaska www.uaf.edu/coop-ext/publications/freepubs/HCM-04956.html

Desert Botanical Garden's Desert House
Rainwater harvesting system in Phoenix, Arizona. www.dbg.org

Development Technology Unit
DTU Roofwater Harvesting Programme
School of Engineering, Warwick University, UK
www.eng.warwick.ac.uk/DTU

Dharma Living Systems (Living Designs Group)
Design and installation services with emphasis on sustainability. www.livingdesignsgroup.com

Earthwrights Designs
Rainwater technology and design. ezentrix@aol.com

Fab-Seal Industrial Liners, Inc.
Offers custom fabricated superior liners for lining tanks holding drinking water. www.fabseal.com

Field Lining Systems, Inc.
NSF/ANSI 61 Standard.
www.greatwesternliner.com/potable
water.html

FogQuest
FogQuest is a non-profit, registered
charity dedicated to planning and
implementing water projects for
rural communities in developing
countries. http://www.fogquest.org/

Forgotten Rain LLC
Heather Kinkade-Levario's rainwater harvesting and stormwater
reuse company.
www.forgottenrain.com

FRALO Plastech Mfg., LLC
Blow-mold HDPE below-grade
tanks. www.fralo.net

Gardener's Supply Company
Rainbarrels
www.composters.com/docs/rain
barrels.html

Greywater Treatment Package Systems
www.pontos-aquacycle.com/pontos
/en/company/pontos.html
www.watersavertech.com
www.ecoplay.nl/en/index.html
www.bracsystems.com/contact-
us.html

Greenbuilder Sustainable Building
Sourcebook
Developed by the Austin Green
Builder Program, this sourcebook,
available on the web, contains a
chapter on rainwater harvesting.
www.greenbuilder.com/source
book/rainwater.html

Gutters Direct.com
Answers for all questions about
gutters and downspouts.
www.guttersdirect.com

Harvest H$_2$O
Rainwater resources
www.harvesth2o.com/

Heat Tapes
www.cpsc.gov/cpscpub/pubs/5045.
html
http://extension.missouri.edu/explore
/agguides/agengin/g01408.htm
www.thermon.com
www.heatersplus.com/easy.htm

"How to Assemble Rain Barrels in the
Pacific Northwest Region"
How to assemble rain barrels to
conserve water, save on water bills,
and provide for garden plants during drought, and also where to buy
them.
www.dnr.metrokc.gov/wlr/PI/rain
barrels.htm
www.dnr.metrokc.gov/wlr/PI/Pdf/
cistern-water-saving.pdf

Hydros Group / Desert Rain Systems
Consultants for renewable water
sources. www.thehydrosgroup.com

Innovative Water Solutions, Inc
A full-service water conservation
planning, design, and system
installation firm for commercial
and residential projects.
www.watercache.com

International Rainwater Catchment
Systems Association (IRCSA)
Dedicated to the promotion and
advancement of rainwater catchment systems technology with
respect to planning, development,
management, science, technology,
research, and education worldwide.
www.ircsa.org

Invisible Structures, Inc.
Rainwater crates.
www.invisiblestructures.com

Kitt Peak National Observatory
An entire water source from rainwater harvesting system.
www.noao.edu/kpno

Lanka Rainwater Harvesting
Forum/Roofwater Harvesting
Research Group
Aims to organize a network to collect and share experiences in
rainwater harvesting within Sri
Lanka. Four-partner international
research program, funded by the
European Union and started in
1998.
www.rainwaterharvesting.com

Leaf Beater Systems
An Australian company that spe-
cializes in water catchment and
storage systems and leaf debris
removal systems.
www.leafbeater.com

LeafGuard
Seamless gutter protection system.
www.leafguard.com

Leafslide
Leaf and debris filter inline with downspout.
www.rainharvesting.com.au

Low Impact Development
Information and resources on low-impact development.
www.lowimpactdevelopment.org
www.goprincegeorgescounty.com

National Sanitation Foundation
A nonprofit organization whose Water Distribution Systems Program certifies methods for the treatment of drinking water.
www.nsf.org

Northwest Water Source
Rainwater harvesting design, construction, and component supply company for residential and commercial projects.
water@interisland.net

Oasis Design Consulting
A home-based design and publishing business providing rainwater harvesting information.
www.oasisdesign.net/water/rain harvesting/index.htm

Ozotech, Inc.
Ozone Filtration Systems.
www.ozotech.com

Permaculture
Rainwater harvesting for drylands.
www.harvestingrainwater.com

Pima County Flood Control District
Link to water-harvesting manual and other references.
www.dot.co.pima.az.us/flood/wh/index.html

Pioneer Water Tanks (Australia 94) Pty Ltd
Rainwater equipment, US contact available. www.pwtaust.com

Rainchains.com
Quality rainchains and garden accents. www.rainchains.com

Rainfilters of Texas, LLC
Factory-authorized distributors for WISY filter systems.
www.rainfilters.com
www.wisy.de/eng/eng/products.htm

Rain Harvesting Pty. Ltd.
Rainwater equipment and technology supplier.
www.rainharvesting.com.au

Rain King
Rainbarrels.
www.rainwatersolutions.com

Rainwater Collection Over Texas
Sales, service, systems, and supplies.
www.greenbuilder.com/source book/Rainwater.html

Rainwater Management Solutions
Rainwater Management Solutions provides rainwater harvesting systems for residential and commercial applications.
www.rainwatermanagement.com

Rainwater Recovery Systems, LLC
Smart solutions for water management.
www.rainwaterrecovery.com

Rain Gardens in Connecticut: A Design Guide for Homeowners.
A residential design guide for rain gardens.
University of Connecticut
www.sustainability.uconn.edu/

Rainsaver
Rainbarrels.
www.rainsaverusa.com

Rocky Mountain Institute
Article and contacts on rainwater harvesting.
www.rmi.org/sitepages/pid287.php

SafeRain
Water diverters.
www.saferain.com.au

Save the Rain
"Save the Rain is an independent nonprofit and is not affiliated with any religious organization. We are simply a group of regular people who decided that the present water conditions in the world are unacceptable and we came together to change it." www.savetherain.org.

Spec-All Products, Inc.
Metal tank supplier and installer.
www.specallproducts.com

Stormceptor
The Stormceptor System CD-ROM user's guide.
www.stormceptor.com

Suntree Technologies
Nutrient-separating baffle box.
www.bafflebox.com

Tank Town
Rainwater collection. Collect rainwater, filter it, and enjoy the finest and healthiest water in the home.
www.rainwatercollection.com/

Texas Guide to Rainwater Harvesting
Texas Water Development Board's comprehensive manual on rainwater harvesting.
www.twdb.state.tx.us/publications/pub.asp

Texas Metal Cisterns
Experts for design, installation and service of rainwater collection systems.
www.texasmetalcisterns.com

Timber Tanks
Selling aesthetically pleasing wooden potable water tanks.
www.timbertanks.com

ToolBase Services
Rainwater harvesting technology inventory (search for Rainwater Harvesting).
www.toolbase.org/

Tucson, City of, Water Harvesting Guidance Manual.
This manual describes a process for evaluating site characteristics and for developing integrated designs in which water harvesting enhances site efficiency, sustainability, and aesthetics. Water harvesting principles, techniques, and configurations are described, followed by example designs for a subdivision, commercial site, public building, and public right-of-way.
http://dot.ci.tucson.az.us/stormwater/education/waterharvest.htm

University of Arizona Water Resources Research Center
Academic water-related information with link to Water Conservation Alliance of Southern Arizona (CASA).
www.ag.arizona.edu/azwater

University of Hawaii
"Rainwater Catchment Guidelines"
www.ctahr.hawaii.edu/oc/freepubs/pdf/RM-12.pdf

University of Newcastle Upon Tyne
A site search will bring several articles on rainwater harvesting.
www.ncl.ac.uk

Water Magazine
A site search will bring several articles on rainwater harvesting.
www.watermagazine.com

Water Tanks.com
Supply company for potable and nonpotable water tanks.
www.watertanks.com

Wonder Water Rain Water Catchment
Wonderwater has one objective: to create a supplemental supply of water so we will continue to have enough to drink, wash, cook, grow, and play in. We accomplish our goal with a 3,000-year-old practice—catching, storing and using the rain.
www.wonderwater.net

3P Technik UK Limited
Rainwater equipment, US contact available.
www.3ptechnik.co.uk

2020 Engineering
Rainwater and stormwater solutions.
www.2020engineering.com

Appendix B:
Metric Conversion Tables

Here are some handy conversions for measurements:

If you know:	Multiply by:	To Find:
Inches	25.4	millimeters
Inches	2.54	centimeters
Feet	0.3048	meters
Yards	0.9144	meters
Miles	1.609	kilometers
Fluid ounces	28.4	milliliters
Gallons	4.546	liters
Ounces	28.350	grams
Pounds	0.4536	kilograms
Short tons	0.9072	metric tons
Acres	0.4057	hectares
Square inches	6.452	square centimeters
Square yards	0.836	square meters
Cubic yards	0.765	cubic meters
Square miles	2.590	square kilometers
Millimeters	0.039	inches
Centimeters	0.39	inches
Meters	3.281	feet
Meters	1.094	yards
Kilometers	0.622	miles
Milliliters	0.035	fluid ounces
Liters	0.220	gallons
Grams	0.035	ounces
Kilograms	2.205	pounds
Metric tons	1.102	short tons
Hectares	2.471	acres
Square centimeters	0.155	square inches
Square meters	1.196	square yards
Cubic meters	1.307	cubic yards
Square kilometers	0.386	square miles

Glossary

Acre-foot (a.f.) – The amount of water needed to cover an acre of land one foot deep. Equal to 325,851 gallons.

Aerobic zone – An area that supports organisms that exist only in the presence of oxygen.

Algae – Aquatic one- or multi-celled plants without true stems, roots, or leaves but containing chlorophyll. Algae can produce taste and odor problems in stored rainwater.

Alluvium – Debris from erosion, consisting of some mixture of clay particles, sand pebbles, and larger rocks. Usually a good porous storage medium for groundwater.

Anaerobic zone – An area that supports organisms that are active in the absence of free oxygen.

Aquifer – One or more geologic formations containing enough saturated porous and permeable material to transmit water at a rate sufficient to feed a spring, or for economic extraction by a well.

Aquifer compaction – The compression of soil that occurs when soil particles fall closer together because of diminished space between them: a result of the withdrawal of aquifer water that fills the voids between grained soil sediment.

Arid or semi-arid environment – Areas in which the ratio of annual precipitation to evapotranspiration falls within the range of 0.05 to 0.65 percent. Excludes polar and sub-polar regions.

Artificial recharge – The act of deliberately adding water to a groundwater aquifer. Artificial recharge can be accomplished by injection wells, spreading basins, or in-stream projects.

Augmentation – Supplementation of the water supply by the importation of water from another supply source such as a municipal water service or from a basin or other source of stored water. Also referred to as alternate water supply or make-up water.

Chlorine – A chemical commonly used to disinfect water. It is highly effective against algae, bacteria, and viruses, but not protozoa.

Cistern – A facility for storing water. A cistern must be closed and placed underground or made of a material that will prevent sunlight from reaching the stored water.

Coliform bacteria – A common bacteria, found in soil and water, that grows in the intestines of warm-blooded animals. Generally not harmful, but high levels may indicate the presence of other harmful bacteria or viruses.

Cone of depression – A drop in the water table around a well or wells that have been pumping groundwater. Depending on the rate of pumping and aquifer characteristics, a cone of depression can be shallow and extend only a few feet, or it can extend for several miles. Since water flows downhill underground, a cone of depression pulls water from the surrounding area, affecting adjacent water tables.

Debris – Any large items that could clog a rainwater system, specifically pumps and irrigation emitters. Debris may include leaves, branches, trash, or cigarette butts.

Desalinization – The process of removing salts and other dissolved minerals from water.

Diversion – A channel that diverts water to sites where it can be used or disposed of through a stable outlet.

Drip irrigation – The application of water directly to the root zone of a plant at a rate slow enough to allow the soil to absorb it without runoff.

Dry well – A large infiltration trench for runoff, typically a vertical trench or narrow hole covered with a filter for debris and oil.

Effluent – A liquid that enters the environment from a point source such as a sewage treatment or industrial plant.

Erosion – Detachment and movement of rocks and soil particles by gravity, wind, and water.

Evaporation – The changing of a liquid to a gas.

Evapotranspiration – The amount of water transpired by vegetation through pores and evaporated.

Filtration – The process of passing water through porous material to strain out particles. Filtration can remove microorganisms, including algae, bacteria, and protozoa, but not viruses.

First-flush device – A container that collects and disposes of the initial rain that falls on a catchment surface, removing both debris and soluble pollutants.

Fissure – A tear in the earth's crust due to land subsidence.

Flocculation – The clumping of particles in water that collide because they fall at different rates. The larger particles that form fall or settle more quickly than the original particles.

Floodplain – The area near a watercourse that becomes inundated during floods. A 100-year floodplain is one that would be inundated by a flood that has a one-in-one-hundred probability of occurring in any year.

Foul flush – A first flush that has been allowed to stand, causing the accumulated debris to rot, which results in polluted and stinking water.

GPCD (Gallons per capita per day) – The average amount of water used by an individual each day. Total GPCD is calculated by dividing total water use in an area, including industrial and commercial uses, by the number of users. Residential GPCD is calculated in the same way, but only considering domestic water use.

Greywater – Water that is collected from baths, showers, washing machines, and sinks (water from kitchen sinks is not allowed to be treated like rainwater).

Groundwater – The water that fills or saturates the spaces between soil particles and throughout porous bedrock such as limestone, sandstone, or basalt.

Groundwater basin – An area enclosing a relatively distinct hydrologic area of related bodies of groundwater.

Hydrologic cycle – The continual movement of water between the earth and the atmosphere through evaporation and precipitation.

Infiltration rate – The rate at which soil will absorb water. Expressed in inches per hour.

Irrigation district – A political entity created to secure and distribute water supplies. Some irrigation districts have departed from their original purpose of providing water for farm irrigation and now primarily serve municipal customers.

Land subsidence – The lowering of the earth's surface due to compaction in aquifers that results from the lowering of the water table.

Municipal water use – All non-irrigation uses of water supplied by a city, town, private water company, or irrigation district. Municipal water use encompasses domestic, commercial, public, and some industrial uses.

Nanofiltration (NF) — A form of filtration that uses membranes with larger pores than reverse osmosis (RO) filtration. NF removes most salts, pathogens, and organics. Like RO, the process requires pre-treatment of water with chemicals or a sand-based system. NF has not been used commercially on a large scale for drinking water.

Natural recharge – Natural replenishment of an aquifer from sources such as snowmelt and storm runoff.

Overdraft – That quantity of water pumped in excess of the replenishable supply or the act of drawing from a water supply or aquifer in amounts greater than replenishment. Also, the sustained extraction of groundwater from an aquifer at a rate greater than its recharge rate, resulting in a drop in the level of the water table.

Paradigm – A way of thinking about and analyzing problems that has become a standard.

Particulates – Solid particles or liquid droplets suspended or carried in the air.

Parts per million (ppm) and parts per billion (ppb) – A measure of the concentration of materials in a liquid, often used to describe the degree of contamination of water. One ppm indicates that for each one million units of water there is one unit of the contaminant. One ppb indicates that for each one billion units of water there is one unit of the contaminant. 1 ppm is approximately equal to 1 mg/L.

Percolation – The downward movement of water in soil.

Permeability – A measure of the relative ease with which a porous medium can transmit a liquid under a potential gradient.

pH – A number from 1 to 14 used to designate the acidity or alkalinity of a soil. Below 7 is increasingly acid, 7 is neutral, and above 7 is increasingly alkaline.

Potable water – Water that is fit for human consumption.

Primary treatment – Initial treatment given to sewage, usually involving the removal of solids and possibly some disinfection. Precedes secondary and tertiary treatments.

Rain – Water that falls as precipitation from clouds in the sky. Considered the first form of water in the hydrologic cycle.

Recharge – Augmentation of groundwater.

Reclaimed water – Water that was used and then purified to a tertiary-treatment level, which allows it to be used on turf or certain other facilities.

Renewable natural resource – A source of energy that can be replenished in a short period of time.

Reservoir – A facility for storing water. A reservoir may be open or covered.

Reverse osmosis (RO) – A process whereby water is forced though porous membranes that filter out solids. RO removes microorganisms, organic chemicals, and inorganic chemicals, producing very pure water. However, the process rejects more water than it filters.

Runoff – Drainage or flood discharge that leaves an area as either surface or pipeline flow.

Secondary treatment – The most common level of treatment of sewage, involving removal of solids, use of bacterial action for purification, and the addition of disinfectants. Follows primary treatment and precedes tertiary treatment.

Sediment – Soil particles and minerals that are washed from land into an aquatic system as a result of natural and man-made activities.

Sewage – Water that has been used by individuals or businesses.

Sewer – A pipeline used to transport sewage to a treatment facility.

Soft water – Water with relatively low concentrations of certain dissolved minerals, principally calcium, magnesium, and iron. Water from which these minerals have been mostly removed, usually through an ion-exchange process. Rainwater.

Subsurface water – All water below the land surface, including soil moisture, capillary fringe water, and groundwater.

Surface water – Water that flows on the surface of the land.

Soil – A naturally occurring mixture on the earth's surface of minerals, organic matter, water, and air that has a definite structure and composition.

Swale – Low areas of land designed into a landscape that capture water and allow it to infiltrate instead of running off the property.

Tertiary treatment – Treatment of water in order to improve its quality to the point where it can be put to a particular beneficial use. Follows primary and secondary treatment.

Tinaja – A naturally existing rock bowl where rainwater collects.

Tohono O'odham – Native American tribe located in south central and southwestern Arizona.

Total dissolved solids (TDS) – A measure of the minerals dissolved in water. Up to 500 ppm is considered satisfactory: A level above that is increasingly unsuitable for domestic use.

Toxic – Describes substances that can cause injury or death when eaten, absorbed through the skin, or inhaled into the lungs.

Turbidity – The reduction of transparency in water due to the presence of suspended particles: a cloudy appearance in the water. Increased turbidity raises the risk of water-borne pathogens growing and reproducing. Because of this, turbid water is more difficult to disinfect.

Underground storage systems – Any vessel located beneath the surface of the earth, such as a watertight concrete tank or corrugated metal pipe, that is useful for holding water.

Urban – An area that has developed a built environment beyond the natural carrying capacity of the land.

Water table – The upper boundary of a free groundwater body, at atmospheric pressure.

Well – A man-made opening in the earth through which water can be withdrawn, with certain exceptions, e.g.: as described in Arizona state law ARS §45-402 (43).

Xeriscape (pronounced "zeer-ih-scape") – A water-efficient landscape design that makes use of low-water-use plants.

Notes

1   Millennium Ecosystem Assessment Board. 2005. *Living Beyond Our Means: Natural Assets and Human Well-Being.* United Nations.

2   Chapagain, A. K. and A.Y. Hoekstra. 2004. *Water Footprints of Nations, Volume 1: Main Report.* UNESCO-IHE Value of Water Research Report Series No. 16. Delft, Netherlands.

3   Falkenmark, M. and J. Rockstrom. 2005. *Rain: The Neglected Resource.* Swedish Water House Policy Brief Nr. 2. SIWI.

4   See 3.

5   Little, Val. 2003. *Graywater Guidelines.* The Water Conservation Alliance of Southern Arizona: Phoenix, Arizona.

6   Gould, John and Erik Nissen-Petersen. 1999. *Rainwater Catchment Systems for Domestic Supply, Design, Construction and Implementation.* South Hampton Row, London: Intermediate Technology Publications Ltd.

7   Pacey, Arnold and Adrian Cullis. 1996. *Rainwater Harvesting, the Collection of Rainfall and Runoff in Rural Areas.* Southampton Row, London: Intermediate Technology Publications.

8   Wahlin, Lars. 1997. *Ethnic Encounter and Culture Change,* ed. Sabour and Vikor. 1997: 233-249.

9   See 8.

10 Winterbottom, Daniel. 2000. "Rainwater harvesting, an ancient technology—cisterns—is reconsidered." Landscape Architecture. April 2000: 40-46.

11 See 6.

12 See 10.

13 See 6.

14 Wilson, Alex. 1997. "Rainwater Harvesting." *Environmental Building News.* May 1997: 1, 9-13.

15 Boers, Th.M. 1994. *Rainwater Harvesting in Arid and Semi-Arid Zones.* Publication 55. Wageninge, the Netherlands: International Institute for Land Reclamation and Improvement.

16 Schemenauer, Robert S., Pilar Cereceda, and Pablo Osses. 2005. *Fog Water Collection Manual.* FogQuest and Margarita Canepa: Thornhill, Ontario.

17 Texas Water Development Board. 2005. *The Texas Manual on Rainwater Harvesting, Third Edition.* Austin, Texas.

18 Centre for Science and Environment. 2000. *A Water Harvesting Manual For Urban Areas, Case Studies From Delhi.* Faridabad, India: Age of Enlightenment Publishers.

19 Manson, D. Brett. 2001. *Reducing Mixing Effects in Water Storage Tanks.* www.eng.warwick.ac.uk/DTU/pubs/rn/rwh/uqpoo2_mason.pdf (15 Sept. 2002).

20 Banks, Suzy and Richard Heinichen. 1999. *Rainwater Collection for the Mechanically Challenged.* Dripping Springs, Texas: Tank Town Publishing.

21 See 17.

22 Agua Del Sol International. 1998. *Water Line.* www.zekes.com/~agua delsol/waterline.htm (27 April 2001).

23 Roofwater Harvesting Research Group. *Styles of Roofwater Harvesting.* www.eng.warwick.ac.uk/DTU/rainwaterharvesting/stylesofr-wh.html (10 November 2000).

24 Hartung, Hans. 2002. *The Rainwater Harvesting CD.* Weikersheim, Germany: Margraf Publishers.

25 Buttle, Mark, Michael Smith, and Rod Shaw. Unknown. *Technical Brief No. 62. Emergency Water Supply in Cold Regions.* Water and Environmental Health at Loughborough (WELL), Loughborough University: www.lboro.ac.uk/well/ (18 August 06).

26 Barr Engineering Co. 2001. *Urban Small Sites BMPs for Cold Climates.* Bar Engineering: Minnesota Council Environmental Services, Minnesota, USA.

27 See 26.

28 See 25.

29 See 25.

30 See 25.

31 See 25.

32 See 25.

33 See 25.

34 Pope, Tim (Northwest Water Source). 2002. Interview with author.

35 AquaEst International. 2004. Personal communication from owner Willem P. Boelhouwer: cleanwater@aquasure.nl.

36 See 17.

37 Beers, Stephen K. 1998. "Sourcing Water from the Sky." www.edcmag.com/CDA/Article Information/features/BNP__Features__Item/0,4120,19385,00.html (15 March 2001).

38 See 6.

39 Program on Conservation Innovation at the Harvard Forest. 2004. *The Report on Conservation Innovation.* Fall 2004. Belmont, Maine: Harvard University.

40 See 39.

41 Ford Motor Co., 2005. "Ford Rouge Visitor Center." www.ford.com/en/company/about/sustainability/2005-06/envReview BuildingsLEED.htm#frvc (3 November 2006)

42 McKenzie, Heidi and Mark E.Holland. 2004. "Sustainable Storm Water Management at the Ford Rouge Complex Redevelopment Site." Internal paper.

43 Lenntech. *Water recycling for cooling purposes by means of a cooling tower.* www.lenntech.com/water_reuse_cooling_process_bymeansof_cooling_tower.htm (3 January 2006).

44 Trafton, Anne. 2006. "Beetle Spawns New Material." Massachusetts Institute of Technology: Internet newsletter http://web.mit.edu/newsoffice/2006/beetles-0614.html (18 August 2006).

45 See 16.

46 See 37.

47 Kelly, Stephen. "Rainwater Recycling and Ecology – A Basis For Planning and Design." Landscape Architecture and Specifier News: November 2005.

48 See 47.

49 *American Observer.* "Florida Company Unveils Disaster-Relief Tool that Plucks Drinking Water from Dry Air." The American University School of Communication's Graduate Journalism Program. www.americanobserver.net/2006/10/05/florida-company-unveils-disaster-relief-tool-that-plucks-drinking-water-from-dry-air/

50 Stevenson, John, *Time for Kids*, World Report Edition, December 8, 2006. Vol. 12 No. 12, New York, New York.

51 See 49.

52 See 49.

Index

FogQuest water tank, 201
Ford, Henry, 134
Ford Motor Company
    Rouge Factory, 134
    Visitor Center, 135-136
Fort Worth Botanical Gardens, 35
Franklin, Benjamin, 99, 131
French drains, 48, 54, 58, 63
freshwater, xiii, 2- 4
freshwater footprint, 2

G

Georgia, University of
School of Environmental Design, xii
Giaradia, 30
Gould (G&L) pump, 139
Graf Universal filter system, 115, 120-121
grains of moisture, 189-190, 192
    see also condensate
Grand Prairie Animal Shelter, 128, 130
Grand Prairie, City of (TX), 128
green roof, 134-135, 172, 177, 214
Green Streets Project, 49-53
green water, 2, 4, 13, 48
greywater, xvi, 2, 99, 111, 204
reuse of, 4, 203, 214
greywater systems, 100, 110, 112, 202-203
groundwater, 2, 12-13, 171
Grundfos pump, 95
Grundfos SQE Submersible System, 121
Guelph, University of, 213
gutters, 65-66, 68-71, 79, 148, 165
as catchment areas, 86, 95, 133
guzzlers, 205-210

H

Harvesting Rainwater for Wildlife, 206
Hawaii Volcanoes National Park, 142
Hayward Power-Flo II, 111
HEB store (Austin, TX), 3
Heritage Middle School (NC), 149
Hilo Board of Trade, 143
hydrologic cycle, 11, 48, 212, 215
Hydromatic HE-20 Submersible system, 115, 120
Hydros Group, 115, 120-121

I

Innovative Artist-Made Building Ports
    Registry, 171
intensity of use (of rainwater harvesting
    system), 34, 36
International Rainwater Catchment
    Systems Association, xi
irrigation, 1, 3, 7, 12, 52, 58, 62, 128,
    150, 162
    see also landscape irrigation
irrigation systems, 25, 112, 131, 133,
    156, 195
    gravity feed, 114
Island Wood School (Seattle, WA), 3

J

J.J. Pickle Elementary School, 147
Jack Nicklaus Signature golf courses, 120
Jade Mountain, Inc. (Boulder, CO), 110

K

Kaibab Guzzler, 206
Kearney residence (Tucson, AZ), 107
Kilauea Military Camp (KMC) (HI),
    142, 143
King County Department of
    Transportation (WA), 171
King Street Center, 171, 173
Kitt Peak National Observatory
    (KPNO), 142, 157

L

L.F. Manufacturing, Inc., 131
Lady Bird Johnson Wildflower Center
    (Austin, TX), 131, 133
Landscape Architecture magazine, 103
landscape drip-irrigation, 176
    see also drip-irrigation systems,
    landscape irrigation
landscape irrigation, xvi, 2, 7, 24-25, 27,
    30, 32, 39-40, 72, 112, 114, 126,
    139, 142, 147, 162, 168, 171, 181,
    183, 193, 199, 202-203, 214
landscape retention basin, 48, 50
landscape swales, 13, 33, 47
    see also swales
Langston-Brown Community Center,
    151
Langston High School (VA), 151
Latent Cooling Load, 185

About the Author

HEATHER KINKADE-LEVARIO'S passion for rainwater harvesting began as a way to create a sustainable component for commercial developments that were lacking in any such elements. She has worked with water collection through her Land Use Planning and Landscape Architectural profession with ARCADIS, as a student working on her Ph.D. in Urban Geography and Sustainability, and as the 2005-2007 President of the American Rainwater Catchment Systems Association (ARCSA), and has published multiple rainwater collection details in McGraw Hill's 2002 *Time-Saver Standards for Urban Design* and in Wiley's 2006 *Time-Saver Standards for Landscape Architecture.* Her writing has appeared in *Landscape Architecture Magazine,* and she is the author of a previous book, *Forgotten Rain Rediscovering Rainwater Harvesting,* which won both a state award and a national award in communication from the American Society of Landscape Architects.

If you have enjoyed *Design for Water*
you might also enjoy other

BOOKS TO BUILD A NEW SOCIETY

Our books provide positive solutions for people who want to
make a difference. We specialize in:

Environment and Justice • Conscientious Commerce
Sustainable Living • Ecological Design and Planning
Natural Building & Appropriate Technology • New Forestry
Educational and Parenting Resources • Nonviolence
Progressive Leadership • Resistance and Community

New Society Publishers

ENVIRONMENTAL BENEFITS STATEMENT

New Society Publishers has chosen to produce this book on recycled paper made with
100% post consumer waste, processed chlorine free, and old growth free.

For every 5,000 books printed, New Society saves the following resources:[1]

35	Trees
3,160	Pounds of Solid Waste
3,477	Gallons of Water
4,536	Kilowatt Hours of Electricity
5,745	Pounds of Greenhouse Gases
25	Pounds of HAPs, VOCs, and AOX Combined
9	Cubic Yards of Landfill Space

[1]Environmental benefits are calculated based on research done by the Environmental Defense Fund and
other members of the Paper Task Force who study the environmental impacts of the paper industry.

For a full list of NSP's titles, please call **1-800-567-6772** *or check out our website at:*

www.newsociety.com

NEW SOCIETY PUBLISHERS